# Did I Really Say That?

# Did I Really Say That?

MUSEUM
SELECTION

First published in 2003
Reprinted for Museum Selection in 2014


Copyright © Complete Editions


Packaged by Susanna Geoghegan Gift Publishing
Typeset by David Onyett


Printed in China

# Contents

# Introduction

It's part of human nature that we sometimes say things we don't mean – or wish we hadn't said at all. Occasionally we are caught out making a prediction which leaves us looking foolish. But for the majority of us, such gaffes and daft predictions stay in the comforting obscurity of our friends and family.

In *Did I Really Say That?* we see the other side of the story; the rich, famous, notorious or just plain daft public figures whose recklessness with the tongue has been immortalised in print. It may be a scientist who goofed over what might or might not happen in the future, or a businessman who failed to foresee the next big thing. Maybe it's a critic who lambasts the latest film – only for it to become a runaway success, or a politician who can't quite get the words out as intended. Or perhaps it's the hapless sports commentator who opens his mouth and manages to put his size twelve feet right in it.

All these public gaffes are fair game for this lively, amusing and irreverent book. It's our chance to get one back on the experts and our opportunity to revel in the misfortune of the Great and the Good.

Laughing at the clangers of others may not be one of the greatest virtues of humankind. but as *Did I Really Say That?* shows, it can be a lot of fun.

# Future Imperfect

*The ability to tell what gadget will work and what won't should be one of the skills of scientists and technicians. Sometimes they get it right; sadly for them, when they do hardly anyone notices. But when they get it wrong, they can get it very wrong, and then we are all on hand to heckle from the sidelines. It may be that experts are just too cautious sometimes, and fail to see the coming trend. Or occasionally they are just so optimistic they get carried away by the cleverness of their thinking. Either way, it can make for cringe-making and sometimes tragic blunders.*

That old curmudgeon Dr Samuel Johnson was underwhelmed by the beginnings of modern aviation on 21 November 1783 when the Montgolfier brothers sent up the first manned balloon flight, a 20-minute journey above Paris. The following year he remarked: 'We know a method of mounting into the air, and I think are not likely to know more…'

Ever heard of the Wankel non-piston engine? No, nor have many people. Yet in the 1960s its invention caused at least one journal to declare: 'The reciprocating piston engine is as dead as a dodo.' And General Motors, who perhaps should have known better, said: 'The Wankel will eventually dwarf such major post-war technological developments as xerography, the Polaroid camera and colour television.' It sank without trace.

In a burst of enthusiasm, the social reformer May E. Lease predicted in 1893 that within a hundred years: 'We will hold communication with the inhabitants of other planets, and Sunday excursions to the mountains of the moon will not excite comment.'

Much was expected of the airship R 101. Not long before its first commercial flight in October 1930 Lord Thomson of Cardington said: 'People are always asking me to give a name to R 101. I hope it will make its reputation with that name.' Sadly it did. The giant airship crashed in October 1930 at Beauvais, near Paris, en route from Britain to India. Forty-seven people perished in the tragedy – just seven survived – and the name R 101 has been etched on the public memory ever since, synonymous with disasters.

Sometimes predictions are spot on – but just a little late. Motorist George Brown from Austin, Texas, received a letter in 1972 from General Motors telling him that they were recalling all 1972 Vega cars because of a fault which meant the rear axle could 'disengage'. Mr Brown decided to follow the advice and drove his car to the company where he had purchased it. On the way, guess what – the rear axle fell off.

The veteran sea captain E. J. Smith spoke in 1907 about his many years at sea and insisted he had led an uneventful life. 'I have never been in any accident of any sort worth speaking about ... nor was I ever in any predicament that threatened to end in disaster of any sort. I am not very good material for a story.' His last voyage before retirement came just five years later when in April 1912 he was in command of RMS *Titanic*. Captain Smith went down with the ship. The *Titanic* itself had been declared practically unsinkable. One of the ship's crew told an onlooker as it stood in the docks: 'God himself could not sink this ship.'

Humans have long looked up at the skies and wondered if they could fly, though in the past few really believed it was possible. This has included some great minds. Lord Kelvin, the Irish scientist, stated with some certainty in 1896 that: 'I have not the molecule of faith in aerial navigation other than ballooning.' Lest no one understood his certainty, he added: 'Heavier-than-air flying machines are impossible.'

A few years later the renowned American physicist, astronomer and mathematician Simon Newcomb was almost

equally clear on the matter. 'Flight by machines heavier than
air is unpractical and insignificant, if not utterly impossible.' To
which he added: 'Aerial flight is one of that class of problems
with which man will never be able to cope.'

◈

The engineer Worby Beaumont, in around 1900, was a little
more open-minded on the subject. Yes, one day humans could
fly, he agreed. 'But the present generation will not, and no
practical engineer would devote himself to the problem now.'
    Well, the Wright brothers Orville and Wilbur clearly
thought different and by 1903 they had managed to get their
little aircraft in the air near Kitty Hawk in North Carolina.

◈

Even after this historic flight there was deep scepticism. Many
newspapers initially refused to print the story on the odd
grounds that it was 'ridiculous'. And the astronomer Simon
Newcomb repeated his doubts, claiming that while one person
might just be carried in an aircraft, it would be out of the
question to carry two at the same time. Impossible, of course,
until the Wright brothers managed just that the following year.

◈

Then again, the sceptics may have had a point. The
Frenchman Henri Mignet was mad about flying and, well, a
little mad as well. He firmly believed that flying was not just for
the elite few, but was for everyone. Which was why he
designed the HM8, a craft kit plane which Mignet boasted that
just about anyone could assemble and fly. The plane, dubbed
the 'Flying Flea' thanks to its unappealing shape, caused a bit
of a stir in the mid-1930s and hundreds of people bought them.
Sadly the plane was less than a success and many never flew at
all. And tragically, Mignet's boast that anyone could fly led to
the deaths of no fewer than eleven would-be pilots.

An early enthusiast for the flying machine was an engineer called Octave Chanute, though even he had his doubts. 'This machine may even carry mail in special cases. But the useful loads will be very small. The machines will eventually be fast, they will be used in sport, but they are not to be thought of as commercial carriers.' Posterity can be forgiving, however. Chanute later had an airfield named after him.

Any book entitled *A Hundred Years Hence* is bound to contain a few clangers, especially viewed after nearly one hundred years. T. Baron Russell was the author of this 1905 tome, and his insight into air travel makes fascinating reading. 'As it is not at all likely that any means of suspending the effect of air-resistance can ever be devised, a flying machine must always be slow and cumbersome,' wrote a cautious Russell. 'But as a means of amusement, the idea of aerial travel has great promise. Small one-man flying machines or the aerial counterpart of tandem bicycles, will no doubt be common enough. We shall fly for pleasure.'

Meanwhile, in Britain, people were still apparently unaware that anyone could fly at all. In 1907, fully four years after the Wright brothers' triumph in North Carolina, the war minister Lord Haldane harrumphed: 'The aeroplane will never fly.' Which may say a good deal about the state of the war minister and the British war machine at the time.

Dr Dionysus Lardner was a highly-regarded scientist of the early nineteenth century, and was, indeed, Professor of natural philosophy and astronomy at University College in London.

However, when it came to predictions about transport his track record was less than inspired. Dr Lardner contended that: 'Rail travel at high speed is not possible because passengers, unable to breathe, would die of asphyxia.'

Now there are many reasons why trains in Britain may not travel at high speed – leaves on the line, the wrong kind of train, and poor track maintenance come to mind – but fear of oxygen deprivation is not one of them. The boffin also thought that mechanically-powered ships would be unable to cross the Atlantic Ocean because the vessels would need more coal to burn than they could carry. This was uttered on the eve of the golden era of steam shipping.

A senior designer at aircraft manufacturers Boeing, Donald Nordstrom, dismissed fears that an aircraft could be brought down by a lightning strike. 'To my knowledge there have never been any fires occurring as a result of such strikes.'

On 8 December 1963 a Pan Am flight heading for Philadelphia was struck by lightning and crashed near Washington DC, killing 81 passengers and crew.

Space is famously known as the final frontier, and for many sceptics it was a frontier too far. The *New York Times* in particular made fun of Professor Robert Goddard, a pioneering scientist who launched the first liquid-fuelled rocket. In 1920 the newspaper scorned the professor's claims that such rockets could work in the vacuum of space and thus pave the way for space travel. It wrote: 'He seems only to lack the knowledge ladled out daily in high schools.'

The US astronomer Dr F. R. Moulton was certain in 1932 that space travel was just a fantasy. 'There is no hope for the fanciful idea of reaching the moon, because of insurmountable barriers to escaping the earth's gravity.' In 1948 the influential *Science Digest* was only marginally more hopeful. 'Landing and moving around on the moon offer so many serious problems for human beings that it may take science another 200 years to lick them.'

At least that was a magazine. The Astronomer Royal, Sir Richard van der Riet Wooley, however, really should have known better. As late as 1956, he declared emphatically: 'Space travel is utter bilge.'

❖

A youthful engineer once showed his plans for a new engine to a senior academic at Cambridge University. 'Interesting work, my boy, but it will never work,' was the instant comment of the learned man. The engineer was Frank Whittle, who patented the basic design for the turbojet engine and paved the way for the first jet planes.

❖

Computers dominate our lives nowadays, but until even quite recently they were regarded with deep scepticism.

Thomas J. Watson, Chairman of the Board of International Business Machines, famously remarked in 1943: 'I think there is a world market for about five computers.' That company is now better known as IBM, one of the leading computer firms in the world. Interestingly, Watson's company motto was: 'Think'.

Meanwhile the cautious verdict of the publication *Popular Mechanics*, discussing the future of technology in 1949, was that: 'Computers in the future will weigh no more than 1.5 tons.'

Then the editor of business books for publishers Prentice Hall stated in 1957: 'I have travelled the length and breadth of this country and talked with the best people, and I can assure you that data processing is a fad that won't last out the year.'

The verdict of Dr Arthur L. Samuel in 1964 was: 'Nor are computers going to get any faster.'

One engineer at the Advanced Computing Systems Division of IBM, talking about the microchip in 1968 asked dismissively: 'But what is it good for?'

Meanwhile Ken Olson, president, chairman and founder of Digital Equipment Corp, said in 1977: 'There is no reason why anyone would want to have a computer in their home.'

Even those who saw the future didn't quite see it big enough. Bill Gates, the billionaire head of Microsoft, was quoted in 1981 on the subject of computer capacity: '640k ought to be enough for anybody.'

In the circumstances we can perhaps understand the fate of Charles Babbage (1792–1871), the English mathematician and astronomer now credited for coming up with the original blueprint for a computer. At his death Babbage's design for an analytical engine was not seen as a practical invention. His posthumous biography stated: 'The extraordinary monument of theoretical genius accordingly remains, and doubtless will for ever remain, a theoretical possibility.'

'This "telephone" has too many shortcomings to be seriously considered as a means of communication. The device is inherently of no value to us.' These were the prophetic words of an internal memo at Western Union in around 1876.

Arthur C. Clarke, the science fiction writer and futurologist, foresaw many things, most notably the development of communications satellites. Yet he was a little hasty about the development of the moon when he wrote in 1975: 'Air-conditioned settlements on the moon will be situated under domes or below ground to avoid solar radiation [by 2000]. Food will be grown in air-conditioned domes and building materials will be mined from the moon itself.'

Clarke was in good company with his vision for the moon – many have predicted the imminent colonisation of the solar system. 'By the year 2000 we will undoubtedly have a sizeable operation on the moon,' said NASA scientist Werner von Braun in 1969. 'We will have achieved a manned Mars landing: and it's entirely possible we will have flown with men to the outer planets.'

In 1967 *The Futurist* magazine stated: 'A manned lunar base will be in existence by 1986.'

Newspaper offices are often visited by people who claim to have important information or to have made a discovery. So it was with a certain weariness and also wariness that a senior editor on the *Daily Express* addressed a junior reporter in 1925 on hearing that a visitor had arrived at the offices that day. 'For God's sake go down to reception and get rid of the lunatic who's there,' said the editor. 'He says he's got a machine for seeing by wireless! Watch him – he may have a razor on him.'

Later that year the 'lunatic' John Logie Baird demonstrated his new invention – something called television.

Cardinal Armand Richelieu was one of the most astute politicians France has ever produced and was the highly influential chief minister to Louis XIII in the seventeenth century. But his understanding of science was less solid. When fellow countryman and scientist Salomon de Daus suggested that steam power was the energy of the future, the statesman was underwhelmed. 'To listen to him you would fancy that with steam you could navigate ships, move carriages; in fact there's no end to the miracles which he insisted could be performed.' Indeed, Richelieu was so irritated by the scientist's claims that he had him put away in a lunatic asylum.

Inventiveness seems an inbuilt human quality, every bit as strong as our determination to organise or to travel. Yet the United States Commissioner of Patents Henry L. Ellsworth was not convinced by this. In 1844 he predicted: 'The advancement of the art [of invention] from year to year seems to presage the arrival of that period when further improvement must end.'

On the subject of patents – we've all heard of the expression 'turkeys voting for Christmas' but why should anyone want to get rid of their own job? That didn't seem to worry the Director of the US Patent Office in 1899, Charles H. Duell, who urged his President, William McKinley (who was later assassinated), to abolish the entire Office. Why? 'Everything that can be invented, has been invented,' was his assured verdict.

The novelist Sir Walter Scott in 1810 took exception to the thought that gas lights might be useful in a major city. 'There is a young madman proposing to light the streets of London – with what do you propose, with smoke?' thundered the writer.

If his father and teachers were to be believed, Thomas Alva Edison, who was born in 1847, was a 'dunce' who would 'never make a success of anything'. Thankfully the great scientist knew otherwise as his string of 1,000 inventions and discoveries – including the electric light bulb – might suggest.

❖

Edison's idea for an incandescent lamp brought a snooty response from a Committee of the British Parliament in the 1870s. It was, thought the Parliamentary geniuses, 'good enough for our transatlantic friends … but unworthy of the attention of practical or scientific men.'

In fact not even all the 'transatlantic friends' (i.e. Americans) were initially impressed by Edison's concept. Henry Morton, President of the Stevens Institute of Technology, summed up the mood when he stated: 'Everyone acquainted with the subject will recognise it as a conspicuous failure.'

❖

When he was at school his fellow-pupils bullied him and one master described him as 'dull and inept'. The object of this scorn? The Scottish engineer James Watt whose development of the steam engine in the 1760s paved the way for the Industrial Revolution.

❖

The Oxford University professor Erasmus Wilson stated loftily in 1878: 'When the Paris Exhibition closes, electric light will close with it and no more will be heard of it.' Meanwhile a German inventor Werner von Siemens said: 'Electric light will never take the place of gas.'

Not that gas had itself always been seen as a viable solution. The English chemist William H. Wollaston said of the proposals to bring gaslight to the capital: 'They might as well try to light London with a slice from the moon!'

When Henry Ford unveiled his first automobile in 1896, onlookers cruelly derided his efforts with the cry, 'Get a horse!'

However the inventor had the last word when no fewer than 15 million of the later Model T vehicle were sold.

At the dawn of the twentieth century a British newspaper article claimed: 'Probably Mr Marconi will succeed in signalling without wires to America from his laboratory at Poole, but the cable companies have no fears – for the rate of transmission in aetheric telegraphy is much slower than where wires are employed.'

The President of the Royal Society from 1890 to 1895 and eminent scientist, Lord Kelvin, was quite blunt about the prospects for broadcasting. 'Radio has no future,' he boldly declared. Lord Kelvin didn't have much time for other scientific breakthroughs either. 'X-rays will prove to be a hoax,' was the view of the learned lord.

Some people need a lot of convincing. In 1932 the author Arthur Lynch observed: 'I am still seeking in fact for anything that Einstein has added to mathematical knowledge.' Another writer, Harold Aspden, was thinking along similar lines in 1969 when he said: 'Einstein's theory is unnecessary.'

There have been some very successful attempts to eradicate certain diseases from human society, but just occasionally experts have been a little quick to announce it. That was the case in 1975 when the World Health Organisation proudly declared that it could reduce its anti-malaria work as, 'malaria has been licked'. Just that afternoon the organisation's Deputy General, Dr Tom Lambo, was rushed to hospital suffering from an illness. Yes, it was malaria.

In 1991 robotics researcher Line Kye said: 'Within five to seven years we will have a lot of service robots cleaning buildings and toilets, or helping out in hotel kitchens. Within ten years ... every home will have them.'

# Did I Say That Out Loud?

*The ability of humans to open our mouths and plant our feet firmly in, is almost limitless. Sadly, it seems a lot of us just can't manage to engage our brain before speaking. There are excuses, for example those social occasions when you simply don't know what to say – and when you do, you really wish you hadn't. And perhaps we should have some pity for those poor sports commentators who have an instant to describe what they are seeing and, sometimes, manage somehow to conjure up an entirely different image. There are many other experts, politicians and writers for example, who really should have known better. But when it came to the chance to open their mouths, they just couldn't resist it. The results can be excruciating, embarrassing, humiliating – and often very, very funny.*

The British Ambassador to Egypt, Sir Miles Lampson, was honoured with the new title of Lord Killearn during his residence in Cairo. At a lunch soon after this happy event, a visitor leant over to the newly ennobled Lord and his wife and confided: 'It's so nice you're here now and not those Lampsons whom everybody disliked so much.'

The acclaimed biographer Michael Holroyd was once at a dinner with a senior member of the Royal Family. The female Royal was showing off her repertoire of accents she could mimic – including northern and Irish accents – with some success. A nervous Holroyd laughed his appreciation out loud, and then guffawed when she started speaking again. 'Do it again, Ma'am,' said the writer. 'That one's priceless.' At this there was a sudden silence during which all the other guests stared at him. The last 'accent' had been the honoured guest's own voice.

At last Prince Charles had got himself engaged, and the whole country was excited at the prospect of his wedding to Lady Diana Spencer. Soon after the happy announcement a Scottish businessman Peter Balfour was in the fortunate position of being able to toast the Prince at a reception for businessmen held in Glasgow. He wished the Prince well, said Mr Balfour proposing the toast to the assembled crowd, and wished Charles a long and happy life with 'Lady Jane'.

Prince Charles had been romantically linked with Lady Jane Wellesley in his younger days.

It seemed like a good idea at the time. Members of the Australian Safety Committee wanted to stage an event to publicise their cause and came up with the idea of a 2,000-mile 'bed-push' from Hobart to Perth. A number of nurses gave up their time for the 1978 event. A spokesman helpfully explained: 'We want to prevent careless accidents.' Sadly, this did not entirely apply to the team of volunteers, as one of them slipped beneath the bed en route and broke her neck.

The playwright William Douglas Home and his wife Rachel had been invited to dinner with some friends. Home arrived separately from his wife as he had been at a play. All went well and at around 11p.m. the playwright and his wife started to leave, at which point the dinner party's host thanked Home's wife Rachel for a 'lovely dinner'. Home was puzzled at this reversal of compliments, until his wife explained that she had brought the dinner herself, as their hosts' cook was away at the time. The playwright could not resist the opportunity. 'In that case, I am at liberty to say that the fish was the most disgusting thing I've ever eaten,' he declared.

There was the briefest pause, before the host replied: 'That was the only dish that I provided…'

According to one newspaper report, a state senator in Colorado state, Mary Anne Tebedo, seems to have found the answer to teenage pregnancies. She is quoted in *The Denver Post* in 1995 as telling the state senate: 'Statistics show that teen pregnancy drops off significantly after age 25.'

A couple called Tim Heywood and Janey Cook were driving back from a party when a tired Mr Heywood fell asleep at the wheel. The flashy sports car veered out of control, went down a hill, hit a pylon and then a steel barrier, before smashing into a wall. The car was a crumpled mess but somehow both of them managed to step out unscathed. 'Thank goodness we weren't hurt,' said Ms Cook with understandable relief. Surveying the wreckage of his pride and joy, Mr Heywood took exception to this comment and slammed what remained of the door in anger. It chopped his finger off.

The captain of a Canadian trawler was understandably elated at the size of the catch his crew had just landed in 1976. In his excitement he immediately radioed home the weight of the catch: '30,000 lb – it's a record.' There was just one small matter the skipper had overlooked – the trawler had a capacity of just 15,000 lb and the boat promptly sank.

That great British actor Sir John Gielgud had a reputation for saying things in social situations without having thought them through first. He was once dining with the Labour Prime Minister Clement Attlee and his family at an hotel. The actor was sitting next to the Premier's daughter and the pair were talking about where they lived. Gielgud remarked: 'I have a convenient home in Westminster, so easy to walk to the theatre. And where do you live?' he asked, throwing back the question to Miss Attlee.

'Number ten, Downing Street,' replied the Prime Minister's daughter.

Another Gielgud classic came when he was having lunch with the actress Athene Seyler and was in a complaining mood. 'I spend all my time in the company of these old bags of stage and screen,' moaned Gielgud. 'Monday, Fay Compton, Tuesday, Sybil Thorndike, Wednesday, Athene Seyler...' Suddenly realising what he'd said, Gielgud quickly added: 'Of course, I don't mean you, Athene!'

The minor peer Lord Portarlington once attended a very lavish reception full of well-heeled guests when he spotted a woman whom he thought looked familiar. Walking up to her with a jaunty air, His Lordship remarked: 'Damn it, Ma'am, I know your face but I cannot put a name to it.'

Queen Victoria was not amused.

We think we know what the politician Hubert Humphrey meant when he was asked to comment on an unsuccessful attempt to assassinate President Gerald Ford. 'There are too many guns in the hands of people who don't know how to use them,' said Humphrey.

The former Liberal Party leader Jeremy Thorpe was once at a reception when a woman approached, and in time-honoured fashion she said: 'You won't remember me...'

At which the politician quickly racked his brain, and replied: 'Of course I do, you're, er, Miss Bag.'

'No,' replied the woman, 'I am Miss Gas.'

The composer and conductor André Previn was having a quiet drink in a London hotel bar when he met a young American composer he knew slightly. The composer joined him for a drink and complimented Previn on a recent performance of his orchestra which he had attended. 'Oh God,' replied Previn. 'That was the night Pollini was supposed to play the Fourth Piano Concerto in the second half but he cancelled, and we were stuck with one of those last-minute substitutions, that really appalling, third-rate lady pianist.' Previn continued: 'I'm really sorry you had to suffer through that!'

The composer gave Previn a look and replied: 'That's all right, I didn't mind. The pianist is my wife.'

David Stockman had the powerful job of Director of the Office of Management and Budget in Ronald Reagan's first term of office. Talking about the administration's budget in 1981, Stockman was quoted: 'None of us really understands what's going on with these numbers.'

He later left the administration to take a job on Wall Street.

BBC commentator Peter West had a knack with words. Talking about the prospects for Jimmy Connors at Wimbledon, West commented: 'Connors' wife is expecting a baby and there was some doubt about his entry.'

His best-known pun was when commentating on the Dutch woman tennis player Betty Stove. 'Miss Stove seems to have gone off the boil,' said an unwitting West.

The British actor Herbert Marshall was making a successful career in America despite losing a leg during the First World

War. He had recently become single again when he encountered John Gielgud at a party. 'Ah Herbert,' said the great man. 'I see you're foot-loose in Hollywood...'

Sometimes a social gaffe isn't the speaker's fault but the translator's. That happened to US President Jimmy Carter during a trip to Warsaw, Poland, in 1978. What Carter told his hosts was: 'I have come to learn your opinions and understand your desires for the future.'

The interpreter translated this as: 'I desire the Poles carnally.'

The occasion was a lunch party given by the Bishop of Coventry and the guest of honour was the then Archbishop of Canterbury Cosmo Lang. A young curate, anxious to talk to such an exalted figure but hopelessly nervous at the same time, stammered: 'Have another piece of Grace, your Cake.'

The late Brian Johnson was a fine cricket commentator who produced some memorable moments of unintentional humour. One of the most famous was during a Test match between England and the West Indies when the English batsman Peter Willey was facing up to the great fast bowler Michael Holding. Or as Johnson put it: 'The bowler's Holding, the batsman's Willey.'

This may have been the same Test match in which the former Test player and summariser Trevor Bailey announced on air: 'I am of course a great Willey supporter.'

On another occasion Johnson was commentating on a side in which Ray Illingworth was captain, and had just taken himself off as a bowler at one end. Or, again, as Johnson had it:

'Ray Illingworth has just relieved himself at the Pavilion end.'

Then there was the time when Johnson was listening alongside his broadcasting colleague Jonathan Agnew, when Ian Botham lost his balance in the middle of the wicket and didn't quite manage to step over the stumps. Or as Agnew told listeners: 'He didn't quite manage to get his leg over.'

Johnson suffered a burst of the giggles which virtually brought the broadcast to a halt.

Mr E. J. Fourie, the new South African Ambassador to Uruguay, may have been a fine diplomat but his geography was lousy. At his first press conference to the media in Montevideo in 1981 he declared: 'I am very happy to be in Peru.'

The Mayor of Chicago Richard J. Daley was talking at a press conference in 1968 when there were riots during the holding of the Democratic Party Convention. He told the assembled journalists: 'Gentlemen, get the thing straight once and for all. The policeman isn't there to create disorder, the policeman's there to preserve disorder.'

Some of the best one-line gaffes in recent time have come from the Bush political dynasty in America. If George W. Bush inherited the ability to succeed in politics from his father George Bush Snr, he also inherited his father's ability to mangle the English language.

First, a few classics from the first President Bush:

'We're enjoying sluggish times, and not enjoying them very much.' Bush Snr on the economy in 1992.

'If you're worried about caribou, take a look at the

arguments that were used about the pipeline. You'd say the caribou would be extinct. You've got to shake them away with a stick. They're all making love lying up against the pipeline and you got thousands of caribou up there.' Bush Snr, speaking in 1991 about the Alaskan pipeline.

'These, they're very dangerous. They trap you. Especially these furry ones … it's these furry guys that get you in real trouble. They can reach out and listen to something – so keep it respectful here.' Bush Snr, speaking to Arnold Schwarzenegger in 1991 about the need to be careful when speaking near open microphones.

'It has been said by some cynic, maybe it was a former president, "If you want a friend in Washington, get a dog." Well, we took them literally – that advice – as you know. But I didn't need that because I have Barbara Bush.' Bush Snr, in 1989 on his wife.

'If a frog had wings, he wouldn't hit his tail on the ground. Too hypothetical.' Bush Snr on life, the universe and everything in 1992.

His son, George W., or 'Dubya', had a hard act to follow – but follow it he did.

'If the terriers and bariffs are torn down, this economy will grow.' Bush Jnr, in January 2000, getting his trade terms muddled.

'The most important job is not to be governor, or first lady in my case,' Bush Jnr, in January 2000, getting his own job and gender muddled.

'The senator has got to understand if he's going to have – he can't have it both ways. He can't take the high horse and then claim the low road.' Bush Jnr, in February 2000 getting his routes muddled.

'It's clearly a budget. It's got a lot of numbers in it.' Bush Jnr in May 2000, clarifying his stance on high finance.

'Rarely is the question asked: Is our children learning?' Bush Jnr in January 2000, clarifying his stance on education.

Prince Philip is not just a senior member of the Royal Family and married to the Queen. He is also, on his own admission, adept at the occasional verbal gaffe. Here's a selection of his most memorable.

In 1996 the Duke of Edinburgh caused an outcry among gun law reformers when he said: 'There's no evidence that people who use weapons for sport are any more dangerous than people who use golf clubs or tennis rackets or cricket bats.'

In 1995 he managed to offend a nation when asking a Scottish driving instructor: 'How do you keep the natives off the booze long enough to pass the test?'

Back in 1966 he provoked outrage by saying: 'British women can't cook.'

And the Duke once said during a tour of Canada: 'We don't come here for our health. We can think of other ways of enjoying ourselves.'

At the Sydney Olympics in 2000 the normally excellent BBC commentary team did manage the occasional foot-in-mouth moment.

For example, here's Stuart Storey on a basketball match: 'He dribbles a lot and his team mates don't like it – you can see it all over their faces.'

Samuel Goldwyn is probably best known as a film producer who founded Goldwyn Pictures Corporation in 1917, a company which later became the famous Metro-Goldwyn-Mayer company.

But the Polish-born movie mogul has a second reputation for his unrivalled and unorthodox mixing of English expressions. Here is a selection of some of the best:

'An oral contract isn't worth the paper it's written on.'

'Gentlemen, include me out.'

'I don't want yes-men around me. I want everyone to tell the truth, even if it costs them their jobs.'

'Anyone who goes to a psychiatrist ought to have his head examined.'

'Give me a couple of years, and I'll make that actress an overnight success.'

'In two words: impossible.'

'True, I've been a long time making up my mind, but now I'm giving you a definite answer. I won't say yes, and I won't say no – but I'm giving you a definite maybe.'

'Let's have some new cliches.'

'Why did you do that? Every Tom, Dick and Harry is named Sam!' Goldwyn's response when a friend told him he had named his son Sam.

'Never make forecasts, especially about the future.'

'Put it out of your mind. In no time, it will be a forgotten memory.'

❖

Jim Scheibel, mayor of St Paul, Minnesota, once answered his own question in public when he asked: 'I'm not indecisive. Am I indecisive?'

❖

A US Senator named William Scott was having an important briefing when one of the officials began talking about missile silos. 'Wait a minute! I'm not interested in agriculture,' said the senator presumably thinking of grain silos. 'I want the military stuff.'

＊

Murray Walker, the Formula One motoring commentator, came up with a few classic gaffes in many years of broadcasting excellence:

'That's the first time he had started from the front row in a Grand Prix, having done so in Canada earlier this year.'

'This is an interesting circuit because it has inclines. And not just up, but down as well.'

'And there's no damage to the car. Except to the car itself.'

＊

Don Zimmer, manager of the Chicago Cubs baseball team, was realistic about his team's season, after their results stood at won four, lost four. 'It just as easily could have gone the other way,' he explained.

＊

The Hollywood actress Brooke Shields once revealed to a grateful world: 'Smoking kills. If you're killed, you've lost a very important part of your life.'

＊

Dan Quayle, a former senator and Vice President to George Bush Snr, enjoyed a fine reputation for putting his political foot in it. Here are a few of his best utterances:

'Hawaii has always been a very pivotal role in the Pacific. It is in the Pacific. It is a part of the United States that is an island that is right here.'

'What a waste it is to lose one's mind. Or not to have a mind is being very wasteful. How true that is.'

'I believe we are on an irreversible trend toward more freedom and democracy – but that could change.'

'If we do not succeed, then we run the risk of failure.'

'We have a firm commitment to NATO. We are a part of NATO. We have a firm commitment to Europe. We are a part of Europe.' Quayle's geographical confusion while explaining America's view of the world.

'For NASA, space is still a high priority.'

'One word sums up probably the responsibility of any Vice President, and that one word is "to be prepared".'

'If you give a person a fish, they'll fish for a day. But if you train a person to fish, they'll fish for a lifetime.'

'Votes are like trees, if you are trying to build a forest. If you have more trees than you have forests, then at that point the pollsters will probably say you will win.'

'It's time for the human race to enter the solar system.'

❖

The singer Britney Spears showed she was a true American girl when she revealed what it was she liked best about her tremendous fame. 'I get to go to lots of overseas places, like Canada,' she gushed. The US has a 3,145 mile land border with its northern neighbour.

❖

The President of France, Charles de Gaulle, clearly had a brilliant insight into Eastern politics. He once said: 'China is a big country, inhabited by many Chinese.'

❖

The former Democratic Vice President, Al Gore, who got beaten for the Presidency by George 'Dubya' Bush, certainly shared some of his opponent's talent for verbal gaffes. He once ventured: 'A zebra does not change its spots.'

❖

Frank Rizzo, a former police chief and mayor of Philadelphia, may have been stating the obvious when he said: 'The streets are safe in Philadelphia – it's only the people who make them unsafe.'

❖

The enthusiastic and popular BBC weather forecaster Ian Macaskill, was prone to the odd gaffe. He once declared: 'An end is in sight to the severe weather shortage.'

# It's a Funny Old World

*The world and human society are complex entities, which may explain why we so often make a hash of describing them. For years experts have been taking out their crystal balls and have been trying to predict trends and work out just how life might be in the future. Some of the predictions are peculiar, others just plain daft. Many of them, it appears, are simply wrong. And if trying to predict changes in society is bad enough, then attempting to make sense of human beings and how we might behave in the future seems to have driven some of the experts straight to the borders of madness. Fashion, homes, crime and even the postal service – many have given their opinions on these subjects; few have come up to the mark. Bless them.*

At the end of the nineteenth century the American
businessman John Wanamaker believed that postal charges
would be a thing of the past in a hundred years. 'Free delivery
will be universal,' he said. The US Postmaster General,
Thomas L. James, was only slightly less optimistic. 'The citizens
who live in the next century are not going to pay two cents for
a letter postage stamp,' he said in 1893. 'The price will be
reduced to one cent.'

Another US Postmaster General, Arthur Summerfield,
suggested in 1959: 'Before man reaches the moon your mail
will be delivered within hours from New York to Australia by
guided missiles. We stand on the threshold of rocket mail.'

Not everyone has foreseen the dangers of drugs that we see
now. As long ago as 1884 the psychiatrist and pioneer of
psychoanalysis Sigmund Freud was reviewing the effects of a
white powder which came from the coca leaf. The powder
induced 'exhilaration and lasting euphoria – which in no way
differ from the normal euphoria of the healthy person,' wrote
the great man. 'It is soon hard to believe that you are under
the influence of any drug.' Freud was writing about cocaine.

Similarly, at the end of the nineteenth century another drug
was being championed by those in the medical profession. One
reviewer, James R. L. Daly, writing in the *Boston Medical and
Surgical Journal*, said the drug was in many ways better than
morphine. 'It is not hypnotic and there is no danger of
acquiring the habit.' Daly had been writing about heroin.

The *Ladies' Home Journal* predicted some changes in the
English language by the year 2000. Writing in 1900, it stated:

'There will be no C, X or Q in our everyday alphabet – they will be abandoned because unnecessary.' The magazine also considered that after English, Russian would be the most spoken language in the world.

It can be quite hard to predict population growths, but that certainly hasn't stopped people trying. Gregory King, in his 1696 work *Observations on the State of England,* had a stab at it. 'In all probability the next doubling of the people of England will be in about six hundred years to come or by the year of our Lord 2300, at which time it will have eleven millions of people. The next doubling after that will be, in all probability, in less than twelve or thirteen hundred years, or by the year of our Lord 3500 or 3600. At which time the Kingdom will have 22 millions of souls…'

The 2001 census for England alone put the population at 49,138,831.

The acclaimed fashion designer Coco Chanel was less than complimentary about the new miniskirt in 1966. 'It's a bad joke that won't last,' she said. 'Not with winter coming.'

The police in Atlanta, Georgia, once received a tip-off that a bank was to be robbed. Officers duly staked out the branch for some hours, much to the irritation of the local manager. He feared that even the discreet presence of the police was alarming both his staff and the bank's customers and eventually he asked them to leave. Which they did. Within just a few minutes the bank was robbed.

In an article in the *New Scientist* magazine Professor Sir Alister Hardy looked ahead to exciting new food sources for mankind. Writing in 1964 he said: 'I think it likely that before 1984 we shall see huge steam or diesel or perhaps nuclear "artificial whales" gathering the krill [small crustaceans] by the shipload to add to the larders of the world.' Sir Alister added: 'By 1984 the krill may be making the greatest addition to man's food supply of the century.'

Arthur Bird's 1903 novel *Looking Forward: a Dream for the United States of America* saw some interesting changes by the end of the twentieth century. He wrote: 'The businessman in 1999 will take a soup-pill or a concentrated meat-pill for his noonday lunch.' Bird also predicted the end of stairs in our homes. 'Every house [will have] its elevator,' he said.

That great futurologist T. Baron Russell had some interesting thoughts in 1905 on our consumption habits of the future. He declared: 'Such a wasteful food as animal flesh cannot survive; and even apart from the moral necessity which will compel mankind, for its own preservation, to abandon the use of alcohol, the direct and indirect wastefulness of alcohol will make it impossible for beverages containing it to be tolerated.'

Smoking cigarettes is nowadays universally accepted as harmful to a person's health. This was not always the case. Writing in *The Doctor at Home* in 1897, one George Black noted: 'The power of tobacco to sustain the system, to keep up nutrition, to maintain and increase the weight, to brace against severe exertion, and to replace ordinary food, is a matter of hourly and daily demonstration.'

❖

Upon being woken from his slumbers to be told that a fire in a bakery on Pudding Lane was threatening London, the Lord Mayor Sir Thomas Bloodworth declared, 'Pish, a woman might piss it out!' and went back to sleep. That was on 2 September 1666, and within four days the Great Fire of London had consumed 13,200 houses, including 460 streets, and 89 churches.

❖

The prospect of a unified Germany after its split into East and West at the end of World War Two was treated with scorn by experts. The *New York Times* columnist Flora Lewis stated in 1984: 'Any realistic sense of the world today leaves it clear that there isn't going to be any German reunification this century, nor probably in the lifetime of anyone who can read this.'

Closer to home, the Foreign Minister of East Germany, Oskar Fischer, declared: 'The Socialist German Democratic Republic and the capitalist Federal German Republic cannot be merged, let alone reunited. Its is as impossible as bringing together fire and water.'

In the autumn of 1989 the Berlin Wall was demolished, and in the following years the two Germanys were formally reunited.

❖

Readers may have been puzzled by a report in the *International Herald Tribune* which wrote about a study of various contraceptive techniques. The study suggested that the diaphragm was the best method. As the paper wrote: this method held 'no material risks…other than pregnancy.'

An edition of the popular BBC programme *Tomorrow's World* suggested in 1966 that in 30 years' time humans would no longer be eating food but instead would consume pills for an 'all-chemical meal'.

The wonderfully named E. E. Fournier d'Albe happily stuck his neck on the line with his view of the future, *Quo Vadimus?* (*Where Are We Going?*), in 1925. That could have been because he knew he wouldn't be around to find out just how far off the mark his predictions would be. He wrote: 'In a hundred years the unification of the human race will be complete. The earth and the fullness thereof will be under the full mastery of man. All animal, vegetable and bacterial life will be kept within strict bounds in the interests of humanity. The earth will be under one government, and one language will be written and understood, or even spoken, all over the globe. There will still be different races and perhaps allied nations, but travel and commerce will be freed and unfettered, and calamities will be alleviated and dangers met by the united forces of all mankind.' Stirring stuff.

The scientist Desmond King-Hele saw a brave new world of sticky tape and stout footwear by the year 2000. Writing in 1975 he said: 'Adhesive tape will be strong enough to take care of all household repairs, and shoes will last a human lifetime.'

A Belgian doctor once appeared in the dock over allegations concerning a treatment by which he claimed to extend people's lives. Giving evidence, the doctor insisted that he was his own patient and that he was confident he would live for a thousand years. The court deliberated but still found him guilty, handing down an eighteen-month jail term. At this the physician collapsed in the dock with a heart attack and had to be taken unconscious to the nearest hospital.

Plastic plays an important part in our lives, but in 1942 the author John H. Walker thought it would completely take over our homes after the end of the Second World War. Writing in *Popular Science*, he stated: 'We are entering the Plastics Era. Your entire house – walls, woodwork, stairs, doorknobs and almost everything else could be made of plastics.'

Thomas Jefferson, the American statesman, had a gloomy view of what would happen when his country developed large centres of population. 'When we get piled upon one another in large cities, we shall become as corrupt as in Europe, and go to eating one another as they do there,' he said in 1787.

The LSD guru of the 1960s, Timothy Leary, predicted in 1965 that the United States would collapse within 15 years. When by 1980 it clearly hadn't, he responded: 'What is time?'

An Italian criminologist and military doctor called Dr Cesare Lombroso believed in the nineteenth century that he had a foolproof way of telling the good soldier from the bad one. Tattoos. He wrote: 'From the very beginning of my studies I was struck by a characteristic that distinguished the honest soldier from his vicious comrade; the extent to which the latter was tattooed and the indecency of the designs that covered his body.'

It can sometimes be hard to spot the next trend in tourist hot spots. Or at least that was the excuse of the Tourist Board of South Vietnam, who ran an interesting ad campaign of devastating understatement in 1965. 'Come to Vietnam,' it ran, 'for your next vacation. Something different.' Given that war had begun there in 1954 and that the conflict massively escalated in the 1960s, this promise was practically guaranteed.

Maybe some people should stick to what they're good at, in George Bernard Shaw's case writing plays. His views on medicine were certainly a little suspect. In 1944 he declared: 'The medical broadcasters and writers of leading articles still keep repeating like parrots that vaccinations abolished smallpox, though vaccinia is now killing more children than smallpox.'

This was the same Bernard Shaw who once remarked: 'You know, Tolstoy, like myself, wasn't taken in by superstitions like science and medicine.'

Back in 1885, some people were not quite as censorious about drugs as nowadays. A manufacturer claimed: 'Cocaine can take the place of food, make the coward brave, the silent eloquent, free the victims of alcohol and opium habit from their bondage and, as an anaesthetic, render the sufferer insensitive to pain.'

World affairs seemed very simple for the nineteenth-century Frenchman Jean-Paul Richter, who announced: 'Providence has given to the French the empire of the land, to the English that of the sea, and to the Germans that of the air.'

Books, it seems, can make us criminals. At least that was the verdict of one Monsieur E. Caron, the head of education in Paris in 1874. 'Hasn't anyone noticed that the worst criminals have been corrupted, since their infancy, by injurious reading?' he asked. 'Hasn't anyone beheld them, in the course of their trials, confessing that it was sordid literature that dragged them onto the road that fatally ended at prison and at the gallows?'

But for the chaplain at San Quentin Prison in the US, August Drahms, the key to criminal behaviour was all in the eyes. 'The eyes of the habitual criminal are usually small and uneasy,' he wrote in 1900. 'In the homicide they are cold and fixed; in the sexual offender generally light, and projecting in their orbits.'

It's not entirely clear whether he thought it was a good or a bad thing, but British journalist and anthropologist John Langdon-Davies, in his 1936 book *A Short History of the Future* insisted: 'Democracy will be dead by 1950.'

That wasn't the end of Mr Langdon-Davies' remarkable insight into the likely changes in our society. Another one was: 'By 1960 work will be limited to three hours a day.'

In the same timescale, thought the author: 'Abundant new raw materials will make food, clothing and other necessities universally obtainable.'

Meanwhile we are now well placed to assess the accuracy of an even more daring prediction by Mr Langdon-Davies: 'Crime will be considered a disease after 1985 and will cease to exist by 2000 AD.'

The British adventurer and colonialist Cecil Rhodes, who gave his name to Rhodesia, now Zimbabwe, foresaw in 1902 a world in which the British Empire would reign supreme. 'The furtherance of the English Empire for the bringing of the whole uncivilised world under British rule, for the recovery of the United States, for the making of the Anglo-Saxon race but one empire – what a dream!' he declared. 'But yet it is probable.'

Interviewed in 1975, the US teamster (or union boss), Jimmy Hoffa, said confidently: 'I don't need bodyguards.' Perhaps he should have thought again. Within weeks of the interview Hoffa vanished into thin air and has not been seen since.

In similar vein the notorious Jack 'Legs' Diamond, who according to some masterminded the St Valentine's Day Massacre in Chicago in 1929, boasted that: 'The bullet hasn't been made that can kill me.'

Diamond died of a bullet wound in 1931.

An American social thinker, Lewis Mumford held out little prospect of Australia retaining its traditional ties with Britain. In 1932, he predicted that in 50 years: 'Australia will be abandoned to the Japanese by its white inhabitants, who will return to an England capable of supporting by agriculture almost double its present population.'

In a burst of optimism in 1893, an American businessman Terence V. Powderly, made a prediction for the future of the criminal justice in a hundred years' time. The public, he said, would be 'so educated and refined that the confinement and punishment of criminals will occupy but little of the thought and time of the men of 1993.'

Similar hope was expressed by members of the National Education Association of America in 1931. It declared that by 1950 'Crime will be virtually abolished by transferring to the preventive process of school and education the problems of conduct which police, courts and prisons now seek to remedy when it is too late.'

The Rome-based correspondent of the *New York Times* Arnaldo Cortesi filed a significant report in March 1974, announcing the end of organised crime in Italy. 'The Mafia, one of the most picturesquely villainous secret societies the world has ever known, exists no more,' wrote Cortesi. 'After holding absolute sway over Sicily for centuries, murdering, blackmailing, terrorizing ... it has met its fate at the hands of the Fascist Government.'

Unfortunately, no one bothered to inform the Mafia of the fact.

The diary entry of King Louis XVI of France on 14 July 1789 makes interesting reading. 'Nothing' he wrote. That was the day that mobs stormed the Bastille prison in the centre of Paris, heralding the French Revolution. Even after this, Louis insisted that his position, or at least his life, was safe. 'The French people are incapable of regicide,' he suggested. In early 1793 the king met his bloody end, accused of treason, at the blade of the guillotine.

At the end of the Second World War, *Time* magazine held out great hopes that China would be ruled under the democratic leadership of Chiang Kai-shek and his Guomindang movement. It declared in 1945: 'The great fact was clear: Chiang Kai-shek had justified those who had long held that his Government was firmly embedded in popular support, and that given peace it could establish an effective administration in China.' It added: 'Never in modern times had the great nation of 450 million people been so close to an era of peace.'

The following year, the Communists under Mao Zedong were waging a fierce civil war against the Guomindang, and by 1949 Mao had proclaimed the People's Republic of China – while his opponents were forced to flee to Formosa (now Taiwan).

Even then, in 1950, Chiang Kai-shek himself insisted 'we will recover the mainland and that the Communists will be crushed.' This optimism was shared by Henry R. Luce, publisher of the influential *Time* magazine, who in 1952 wrote: 'After Chiang Kai-shek has landed and maintained himself for three months on the mainland, the Communist menace to Asia will be finished and the whole of Asia will turn anti-Communist.'

Over the coming decades Mao increased his hold over China, which still remains communist, and the United Nations and then America fought unsuccessful wars in Korea and Vietnam against the spread of communism.

The Homosexuality Bill of 1965, which was aimed at decriminalising homosexual acts in Britain, met with opposition in some quarters. No less a figure than Viscount Montgomery of Alamein, who as General Montgomery was one of the heroes of the Second World War, declared: 'This sort of thing may be tolerated by the French – but we are British, thank God.'

Homosexuality ceased to be illegal for those over 21 in 1967.

The eminent French anthropologist François Voisin came up
with an explanation for criminal behaviour in a book in 1843.
'Criminal brains are at a minimum of development in their
anterior and superior parts, in the parts that make us what we
are and place us above the animals and make us men,' he
declared. His conclusion, then was simple. 'Criminal brains are
placed by their nature entirely outside the human species.'

The introduction of Prohibition in 1919 was supposed to cure
the evils of alcohol in American society. The law – also known
as the Volstead Act and the Eighteenth Amendment – banned
the making, sale or transportation of alcohol. The official in
charge of the law, Colonel Daniel Porter, said in 1920: 'There
will not be any violations to speak of.'

The British author John Frederick Charles Fuller looked on
admiringly. 'In a generation, those who are now children will
have lost their taste for alcohol,' he wrote in 1925.

The great industrialist of the day Henry Ford, the car
manufacturer, was also optimistic about the law's ultimate
success. 'There are a million boys growing up in the United
States who have never seen a saloon, and who will never know
the handicap of liquor,' he wrote in 1929. 'The abolition of the
commercialised liquor trade in this country is as final as the
abolition of slavery.'

He added for good measure: 'The country couldn't run
without prohibition. That is the industrial fact.'

And as moves began to end Prohibition, US senator Morris
Sheppard declared colourfully in 1930: 'There is as much
chance of repealing the Eighteenth Amendment as there is for
a humming-bird to fly to the planet Mars with the Washington
Monument tied to its tail.'

Prohibition was repealed in 1933, having singularly failed to prevent the making and drinking of alcohol in America.

The Prime Minister of France, Guy Mollet, stated in 1956: 'France will remain in Algeria. The bonds linking metropolitan France and Algeria are indissoluble.'

Six years later, in July 1962, Algeria gained its independence.

# Through a Glass Darkly

*Scientists are important people, and their work often helps transform the way we live. Where would we be now without those who have discovered electricity, explained gravity or understood evolution? Perhaps it's precisely because scientists are so important, and often so infuriatingly sensible and accurate, that we get so much pleasure out of their occasional goofs. After all, scratch the surface of any scientist, and you're likely to find an irrational, envious, stubborn individual just like the rest of us. The difference is, when scientists get it wrong, they often get it spectacularly wrong, which may dismay them – but brings a quiet pleasure to the rest of us.*

❖

Weather-forecasting can be a tricky business, especially when
the stakes are high. That was the experience of the Director of
the Provincial Weather Bureau in Formosa – now Taiwan –
who in 1964 declared that the approaching Hurricane Gloria
would not hit the country. That was just hours before the
storm did arrive – leaving a trail of 239 deaths and $17 million
damage in its wake. The director was later arrested and
charged with negligence but escaped further action after
pleading that he had simply done his best.

❖

The popular BBC weather forecaster Michael Fish told a late
night audience in October 1987: 'A woman rang and said she
heard a hurricane is on the way. Well, if you are watching and
waiting, there isn't.'
     The next day the south of Britain was hit by one of the
worst storms for centuries, which caused widespread wreckage,
killed at least 13 people and brought huge economic
disruption.

❖

The world of science got very excited by the apparent
discovery of the remains of a human giant found by workmen
near the town of Cardiff in New York State in October 1869.
Could this be the body of one of those giants the Bible said
once walked the earth? A professor of palaeontology James H.
Drayton, who led a team of researchers who examined the
remains, declared it: 'The most remarkable object yet brought
to light in this country.' The artist and sculptor Cyrus Cobb,
who thought he knew a thing or two about the human form,
looked at it and stated: 'Any man calling this thing a humbug
brands himself a fool.'

Alas, the ancient 'giant' turned out to be a statue made of gypsum a few months before. It had been buried in a field next to a well by a hoaxer called George Hull who then called in the workmen who unearthed it.

Pollution may now be thought of as one of the biggest issues facing the world, but scientists have not always thought so. A lecturer in physiology in London, L. Erskine Hill, was quoted in 1912: 'Experimental evidence is strongly in favour of my argument that the chemical purity of the air is of no importance.'

One P. Norcott had a fascinating idea to help mankind in his 1970s book *Bigger and Better Earthquakes*. How to avoid the destruction caused by earthquakes? Straightforward, he said. 'The only way to stop earthquakes is to stop the pressure building up in the first place, and this can only be done by keeping the earth at a constant speed.'

The possibility of life on other planets has long fascinated humans. In the mid-1890s the American astronomer Percival Lowell claimed that Mars was inhabited and that Martians had constructed a series of huge canals to protect them against the drying of their planet.

In 1892 the founder of the French Astronomical Society Camille Flammarion suggested: 'The present inhabitation of Mars by a race superior to ours is very probable.'

Sadly, recent space probes to the red planet have failed to confirm either the existence of these wonders of engineering or indeed of a race even equal to our own.

Sometimes it can be hard for a teacher to assess the potential of a pupil. Or at least that must have been the excuse of the sadly unnamed master who once declared to his ten-year-old pupil: 'Einstein, you will never amount to much.'

The Greek philosopher Aristotle, who lived in the fourth century BC, stated categorically: 'The brain is an organ of minor importance.'

When asked to reply to suggestions in 1953 that cars might contribute to pollution, a spokesman for the Ford Motor Company said: 'The Ford engineering staff, although mindful that automobile engines produce exhaust gases, feels these waste vapours are dissipated in the atmosphere quickly and do not present an air pollution problem.'

The Medical Officer to the Institute of Insurance in London, one Dr Linard Williams, had some interesting dietary advice for the population in 1932. He stated: 'If your eyes are set wide apart your should be a vegetarian – because you inherit the digestive characteristics of bovine or equine ancestry.'

The Governor of the US state of Oklahoma, William Murray, stated in 1932: 'It's a scientific fact that if you shave your moustache you weaken your eyes.'

In the nineteenth century scientists warned of the dangers of eating certain foods that could make people – and particularly women – too interested in sex. The American doctor Dio Lewis, author of *Chastity: or, Our Secret Sins*, published in 1874, was especially worried about spicy foods. 'Everything which inflames one appetite is likely to arouse the other also,' he explained. 'Pepper, mustard, ketchup and Worcestershire sauce – shun them all. And even salt in any but the smallest quantity, is objectionable. It is such a goad towards carnalism that the ancient fable depicted Venus as born of the salt sea-wave.'

Well bred women, of course, were not supposed to be much interested in sex at all. This view lingered well into the twentieth century. The Professor of Hygiene at the University of Pennsylvania, Joseph G. Richardson, said in 1909: 'If a woman is normally developed mentally, and well bred, her sexual desire is small.' The good doctor helpfully continued: 'If this were not so, the whole world would become a brothel and marriage and a family impossible.'

Pierre Pachet, Professor of Physiology at Toulouse, stated in 1872: 'Louis Pasteur's theory of germs is ridiculous fiction.'

Pasteur is now regarded as one of the fathers of modern microbiology; he also created the first vaccine for use against rabies.

British surgeon Sir John Eric Ericksen, who was appointed Surgeon-Extraordinary to Queen Victoria, considered there were limits to which any sensible doctor could go in the treatment of patients. He suggested that: 'we have already, if not quite, reached these final limits, there can be little question. The abdomen, the chest, and the brain will forever be shut from the intrusion of the wise and humane surgeon.'

A Mr Darwin once told his son that he was a good-for-nothing who would be a 'disgrace to yourself and all your family'. Admittedly this was some years before the nineteenth-century scientist Charles Darwin published his famous book *The Origin of Species* and its theory of evolution which forever changed the way humans viewed the world.

In the Middle Ages, the author William of Normandy told his credulous audience: 'The lioness giveth birth to cubs which remain three days without life. Then cometh the lion, breatheth upon them. And bringeth them to life.'

Most of us consider the sun to be a bright burning yellow object we see in the sky, but John Timbs, author of *Things Not Generally Known* in 1875, rather thought he knew differently. He opined: 'The most recent observations confirm the supposition that the Sun is a black opaque body, with a luminous and incandescent atmosphere, through which the solar body is often seen in black spots, frequently of enormous dimensions.'

Which led to an interesting question – could the sun in fact be inhabited? To which Timbs replied: '…let anyone ask me if the Sun can be inhabited by beings organised in a manner analogous to those which people our globe, and I hesitate not to reply in the affirmative. The existence in the Sun of a central obscure nucleus, enveloped in an opaque atmosphere far beyond which the luminous atmosphere exists, is by no means opposed, in effect, to such a conception…'

The proposition that the sun could be home to life was not just the preserve of fanciful writers. The German-born British astronomer William Herschel (1738–1822) was a respected scientist, who discovered the planet Uranus in 1781 and two satellites of Saturn. Yet he too stated that the sun could be 'abundantly stored with inhabitants'.

The idea that our sun was a fiercely burning bright object was ridiculed by some as late as the 1970s. The Revd P. H. Francis, in *The Temperate Sun*, argued: 'The notion that the Sun is on fire is rubbish, and merely a hoary superstition, on a par with a belief in a flat earth, an earth resting on the back of a tortoise or an elephant, or a sun revolving around a stationary earth. It rests on no sure basis of evidence; and if it is discarded, great simplification becomes possible in the sciences of astronomy, geology and physics, and many other branches of science can be placed on surer foundations.'

As if to clinch his point, he added: 'If the Sun is a hot body, it is improbable that life on earth will exist tomorrow.'

Not content with completely changing our views of the sun, the Revd Francis also dismissed any suggestion that stars were just suns at vast distances from us; instead they were just a reflection of our own sun on the surface of 'infinity'. As he pointed out: 'No star has a real existence, any more than the image of a candle in a mirror has a real existence.'

George Bernard Shaw was undoubtedly a great writer, but his grasp of science was a little less secure. He once said: 'When astronomers tell me that a star is so far off that its light takes a thousand years to reach us, the magnitude of the lie seems to me inartistic.'

The twentieth-century British novelist D. H. Lawrence, author of *The Rainbow* and *Women in Love*, was equally all at sea when it came to the physical world around him. 'Whatever the sun may be, it is certainly not a ball of flaming gas,' he stated.

The great Thomas Jefferson, the third President of the United States, was decidedly sceptical about the existence of meteors. In 1807 he said: 'I could more easily believe that two Yankee professors would lie than that stones would fall from heaven.'

Even when a scientist makes an important discovery, they don't always grasp its full significance. The great New Zealand-born British scientist Ernest (later Baron) Rutherford was an early pioneer of atomic research and helped the modern understanding of atomic particles. However he was dismissive of the practical value of such a discovery. He used to toast: 'To the electron – may it never be of any use to anyone.' Modern watchers of the telly – the television is just one invention which relies on using electrons – may beg to differ.

More seriously, Rutherford was also unconvinced of the importance of splitting an atom. He said: 'The energy produced by the breaking down of the atom is a very poor kind of thing. Anyone who expects a source of power from the transformation of these atoms is talking moonshine.'

Another sceptic of atomic power was the Nobel Prize winner and American physicist Robert Andrews Millikan, who stated in 1923: 'There is no likelihood man can ever tap the power of the atom. The glib supposition of utilizing atomic energy when our coal has run out is a completely unscientific utopian dream, a childish bug-a-boo. Nature has introduced a few foolproof devices into the great majority of elements that constitute the bulk of the world, and they have no energy to give up in the process of disintegration.'

The Austrian physicist and philosopher Ernst Mach, who died in 1916, had little time for the newfangled ideas of scientists such as Albert Einstein. 'I can accept the theory of relativity as little as I can accept the existence of atoms and other such dogmas,' he said.

And the eccentric American engineer and self-appointed theoretical physicist George Francis Gillette (born 1875) was scathing of much of modern science in general, but had a particular down on Einstein. His comments included: 'Einstein a scientist? It were difficult to imagine anyone more contrary to what a scientist should be... As a rational physicist, Einstein is a fair violinist.'

Gillette also describes relativity as the 'moronic brainchild of mental colic' and even 'voodoo nonsense'.

The author also predicted that by 1940 'the relativity theory will be considered a joke. Einstein is already dead and buried, alongside Andersen, Grimm, and the Mad Hatter.'

Einstein was named 'Person of the Century' by *Time* magazine.

It was 1859, and the Vice Chancellor of Cambridge University Dr John Lightfoot announced confidently that both Heaven and Earth were created at the same time on 23 October, 4004 BC. At 9 a.m., to be precise. Later in the same year Charles Darwin published *The Origin of Species*, which established the now accepted view that the universe has evolved gradually over billions of years.

One Professor Haughton was, however, impatient with Darwin and his theories on evolution and natural selection, put forward in *The Origin of Species*. 'All that was new in them was false, and all that was true was old,' was the learned man's verdict.

Another observer, George Paulin, declared in 1908: 'The geological record shrieks out the most emphatic refutation of Darwin's doctrine of Natural Selection as the evolutionary power of Nature.'

By the 1930s there were still many opposed to the very notion of evolution. Commentator R. C. Macfie said: 'It is scandalous that children and students should be taught as a proven fact that these ancestors were apes, and should be shown abominable pictures of primitive man as a shaggy ape-like creature with a low forehead, receding chin, bowed back and bent legs. Such science is a disgrace to the spirit of science and a crime against humanity: and the Catholics and Daytonians deserve honour for declining to accept a totally unproved hypothesis.'

A twelfth-century book called *The Book of Beasts* contained some remarkable information about one of the largest animals in the world. It declared: 'The elephant's nature is such that if he tumbles down he cannot get up again. Hence it comes that he leans against a tree when he wants to sleep – for he has no joints in his knees. This is the reason why a hunter partly saws through a tree, so that the elephant, when he leans against it, may fall down at the same time as the tree.'

As late as the seventeenth century, scientists believed that the blood of a particular domestic animal had extraordinary powers. The writer Sir Thomas Browne stated: 'A diamond, which is the hardest of stones, not yielding unto steel, emery or any other thing, is yet made soft by the blood of a goat.'

The French philosopher and writer Jean-Jacques Rousseau saw little point in science trying to reduce the huge infant mortality rate of his day. He wrote in 1762: 'One half of the children born die before their eighth year. This is nature's law – why try to contradict it?'

When the great pioneering astronomer Galileo, aided by a telescope, claimed to have discovered in 1610 that Jupiter has four moons, there was widespread scepticism from his peers. Francisco Sizzi, a professor of astronomy, stated: 'Jupiter's moons are invisible to the naked eye and therefore can have no influence on the earth, and therefore would be useless, and therefore do not exist.'

By 2002 no fewer than 39 satellites or moons of the giant planet had been discovered.

Winston Churchill was unparalleled as a war leader, but was prone to the occasional rash statement. In 1932, before his glory years, he made a prediction for the future about science. He suggested: 'Fifty years hence we shall escape the absurdity of growing a whole chicken in order to eat the breast or wing, by growing these parts separately under a suitable medium.'

Some happy scientific advice was given by a Dr S. L. Katzoff, member of the San Francisco Institute of Human Relations, during the Second World War. He noted: 'A genuine kiss generates so much heat it destroys germs.'

The renowned inventor and scientist Thomas Edison was ahead of his time on many things, but his understanding of biology was less well developed. Quoted in *Good Housekeeping* in 1912, the great man suggested: 'Direct thought is not an attribute of femininity. In this, woman is now centuries behind man.'

Just two years later a Professor Hans Friedenthal, from Berlin, expressed his fears should women ever start to use their minds. He said: 'Brain work will cause the new woman to become bald, while increasing masculinity and contempt for beauty will induce the growth of hair on the face.'

His conclusion? 'In the future, therefore, women will be bald and will wear long moustaches and patriarchal beards.'

Perhaps women should just have heeded the views of Sir William Osler, Professor of Medicine at Johns Hopkins University, who said in 1903: 'It is the prime duty of a woman of this terrestrial world to look well.'

The nineteenth-century surgeon and scientist Dr Alfred Velpeau clearly had little time for those wimps who can't bear a little bit of pain during operations. In 1839 he stated: 'The abolishment of pain in surgery is a chimera. It is absurd to go on seeking it.' In 1946 the first successful operation on a patient rendered unconscious by ether was carried out.

# That's Entertainment

*Making predictions in the entertainment industry is riskier than in most other areas of life. The error of your ways is so visible – and so quickly realised. Which may help to explain why sport, music, writing and above all films provide such a rich vein of material for the critical gaffe. What may look like an obvious loser as a film has a nasty habit of turning into a smash hit, leaving the critic with bucket loads of very obvious egg all over their face. Spotting the trends can be tricky too – TV, radio, movies, they've all been roundly dismissed by the 'experts' but stubbornly refuse to go away. The lesson for any budding critic should be: be careful what you say – it might, and probably will, come back to haunt you. Fortunately for us, it seems very few people have taken this sound advice.*

A fine poet, John Betjeman, but a little optimistic when it came to cinema. In 1935 Betjeman enthused: 'Colour and stereoscopy will make the cinema into the greatest art in the world. Bad films will be impossible.'

The great singer Frank Sinatra saw little future for certain types of modern music. He declared in 1957: 'Rock 'n' Roll is phoney and false, and sung, written and played for the most part by cretinous goons.'

Pop stars are not noted for their brains, which may explain the former Beatles drummer Ringo Starr saying: 'I love Beethoven, especially the poems.'

Rock 'n' Roll is now fully ingrained in Western culture but some early observers saw it as a threat to our way of life. A Pentecostal Minister called Revd Albert Carter said the music would 'turn young people into devil worshippers, destroy marriage, create lawlessness and impair nervous stability'. He concluded: 'It is an evil influence on the youth of our country.'

There was a literary dispute in the 1970s over the stories published by one James Tiptree Junior. The dispute was over rumours that Tiptree, whose stories were widely praised, was not in fact a man but a woman writing under a male pseudonym. One writer, Robert Silverberg, was somewhat dismissive of the claims. Writing an introduction to Tiptree's *Warm World and Otherwise* in 1975, Silverberg said the theory was absurd because there was something 'ineluctably masculine' about the author's prose style. Digging a deeper hole he added: 'I don't think the novels of Jane Austen could have been written by a man nor the stories of Ernest Hemingway by a woman, and in the same way I believe the author of the James Tiptree stories is male.'

By 1977 the true identity of Tiptree was revealed: she was Dr Alice Sheldon, a former CIA officer who had kept her identity secret for reasons of national security.

✦

The director Francis Ford Coppola was less than pleased about having to make a certain movie that a film studio was urging him to do. He told his father in 1970: 'I was at Paramount all day yesterday and they want me to direct this hunk of trash. I don't want to do it. I want to do art films.'

Fortunately his father persuaded him to take the job, and *The Godfather* went on to become one of the most successful and critically acclaimed films in history.

✦

A teacher once told the young G. K. Chesterton – who could not read until he was eight – that he had no brain but 'only a lump of white fat' where that organ should be. The youngster went on to become one of Britain's best and most cherished writers.

✦

The writer and social philosopher H. G. Wells, the author of *The Time Machine* and *The War of the Worlds*, had a real gift for peering into the future and understanding the future development of mankind. He even wrote a book in 1933 called *The Shape of Things to Come* which predicted a number of changes that did indeed happen. Yet even Wells had his blind spots. In *The Way the World is Going*, published in 1928, Wells wrote: 'I am reported to be "pessimistic" about broadcasting, though the truth is I have anticipated its complete disappearance – confident that the unfortunate people, who must now subdue themselves to "listening-in", will soon find a better pastime for their leisure.' Which is not quite how things turned out.

The great editor of the *Manchester Guardian* newspaper C. P. Scott, who died in 1932, was noted for his wit and elegance with the written word. 'Television?' he once said. 'No good will come of this device. The word is half Greek, half Latin.'

The novel *Ulysses* by the great Irish writer James Joyce is widely regarded as one of the masterpieces of the English language but it was not always so highly regarded. The critic Gerald Gould, in 1924, could hardly have been more critical. 'The telephone directory is, because of its rigorous selection and repression, a work of art compared to the waste-paper basket. And *Ulysses* is a waste-paper basket,' Gould wrote.

The renowned BBC boxing commentator Harry Carpenter was usually a very shrewd observer of his sport, but had the occasional lapse. During the eighth round of the famous 'Rumble in the Jungle' fight in Zaire between Muhammad Ali and George Foreman in 1974, Carpenter said dramatically: 'There's no way Ali can win this one now.' Within a few seconds the bout was indeed over. Ali had launched a brief, furious counter-attack and had knocked his opponent to the floor, winning in some style.

※

Having touted their idea for a new cartoon character around for five years, Joe Shuster and Jerry Siegel were naturally delighted when finally Harry Donenfeld signed them up for his company Detective Comics Inc. After all, just about every other magazine publisher had rejected the idea. At the time the pair signed a form which gave them $10 a page, but handed over all rights to the firm. In that way the two cartoonists signed away all future film, TV and syndication rights to their creation – *Superman*. Donenfeld was making $100,000 a year out of the strip by 1940.

※

A review in *Blackwood's Magazine* in 1818, penned by a Mr J. G. Lockhart, suggested that on the evidence of the poem *Endymion*, a certain writer would have more success as a chemist – he was a licensed apothecary – than as a poet. The target of his attack, John Keats, is widely regarded as one of the greatest poets in the English language.

Keats seems to have suffered quite a lot from the critics for his art. When confronted with the poet's collected works, the historian and writer Thomas Carlyle regarded it in a fine turn of phrase as 'Fricassee of dead dog'.

※

One of the acclaimed poems of the twentieth century, *The Waste Land* by T. S. Eliot, was dismissed by a critic in the *Manchester Guardian* newspaper as 'so much waste-paper'.

※

In *The Listener* magazine in 1936 Rex Lambert wrote: 'Television won't matter in your lifetime or mine.'

Twelve years later and there were still huge doubts about the importance of this discovery. Radio pioneer Mary

Somerville said in 1948: 'Television won't last. It's a flash in the pan.'

The British Board of Film Censors has not always been noted for its grasp of the finer points of film-making. Banning Jean Cocteau's film *The Seashell and the Clergyman* in 1956, the Board sniffed: 'This film is apparently meaningless – but if it has any meaning it is doubtless objectionable.'

The jury's still out on a prediction made by the pioneering Hollywood director David Wark Griffith in 1924. But readers can judge themselves whether his view that by 2024 the cinema will have helped in eliminating 'all armed conflict' from the world is likely to come true.

The wonderful American poet Walt Whitman wasn't sure if the works of one of the greatest writers in the English language was quite to the taste of his fellow countrymen. 'Shakespeare's comedies are altogether non-acceptable to America and democracy,' he wrote. Whitman was in good company. Another eminent writer, George Bernard Shaw, said of Shakespeare: 'It would positively be a relief to dig him up and throw stones at him.'

The early nineteenth-century critic John Hunt may have had many fine qualities, but it would appear that art appreciation was not among them. Hence his comment: 'Rembrandt is not to be compared in the painting of character with our extraordinarily gifted English artist, Mr Rippingille.'

Rippin-who? Exactly. Though he was a competent artist, the

name of Edward Villiers Rippingille, who died in 1859, now languishes in comfortable obscurity, while Rembrandt is regarded as one of the greatest artists of all time.

The renowned art critic John Ruskin maybe should have known better. Reviewing a painter's exhibition, he wrote in 1877: 'I have seen and heard much of cockney impudence before now; but never expected to hear a coxcomb ask two hundred guineas for flinging a pot of paint in the public's face.' The painter in question was James Whistler, who is now highly regarded as an artist. Whistler in fact sued for libel over Ruskin's comments, but though he won, he received only a token farthing in damages and no costs, which led to great financial hardship.

Dr Samuel Johnson, that brilliant critic, occasionally got it wrong. Writing in 1776 Dr Johnson gave his views on literary trends and stated: 'Nothing odd will do long. *Tristram Shandy* did not last.' The famous novel by Laurence Sterne (1713–1768) first published in the eighteenth century, is still in print today.

A number of experts failed to come to grips with the advent of talking movies in the early twentieth century. The Hollywood studio boss Harry Warner asked: 'Who the hell wants to hear actors talk?'

The film critic Ernest Betts said he was convinced that films 'should be seen and not heard'. Fellow critic A. P. Herbert once wrote of the talkies: 'They are doomed to an early and expensive death.'

And director D. W. Griffith stated in 1924: 'We do not want

now and we shall never want the human voice with our films.'

Meanwhile the inventor Thomas Alva Edison – who perhaps should have known better – was emphatic on the subject. In 1925 he said: 'People will tire of talkers. Talking is no substitute for the good acting we had in silent pictures.' The following year Edison was as certain as ever. 'I have determined that there is no market for talking pictures.'

Elvis Presley is every bit as famous in death as he was in life, but try telling that to some early critics. Comic Jackie Gleason said in 1956 that Elvis 'can't last'. Writing in the *Daily Mail* Jack Payne opined: 'Singing in any form is foreign to Elvis'. While at the same period D. W. Brogan asked through the columns of the *Manchester Guardian*: 'Who will sing "Blue Suede Shoes" ten years from now?' Who indeed?

After his first gig, Presley was fired and told to rethink his choice of career. Jim Denny, booking clerk of the Grand Ole Opry club in Nashville told him in September 1954 : 'You ain't goin' nowhere son. You ought to go back to drivin' a truck.'

No fewer than thirteen publishers turned down the chance to publish a book by then unknown writer Frank Herbert in the 1960s. One called it too slow, another said it was too long. The fourteenth publisher liked the manuscript – and *Dune* went on to be an international best-seller, with more than ten million copies sold worldwide. As one of the thirteen publishers had said in a letter to Herbert: 'I may be making a serious mistake, perhaps the mistake of the decade, but…'

The famously successful Hollywood blockbuster *Gone with the Wind* was not spotted by everyone as an obvious triumph. MGM film boss Louis B. Mayer was told by his chief producer that: 'No Civil War picture ever made a nickel' – though MGM did make the film. The actress Bette Davis scorned the chance to play Scarlett O'Hara, suggesting the movie would be a 'pip', or flop. And even the director, Victor Fleming, turned down the chance to take a share in the takings from the film as part of his payment with the immortal words: 'Don't be a damn fool. This picture is going to be one of the biggest white elephants of all time.'

The actor Gary Cooper also turned down the chance to play Rhett Butler in the movie, saying it would be the 'biggest flop' in Hollywood history. He added: 'I'm glad it's going to be Clark Gable who's falling on his face and not Gary Cooper.'

A soccer writer once confidently asserted that the seventeen-year-old player he had just witnessed would never hold down a regular team place in top-flight football as he lacked big match temperament. Which may explain why the writer remained on a local newspaper. Meanwhile the subject of his comments, one Stanley Matthews, played more than 700 football league matches, won 54 international caps and in 1965 was the first footballer to be knighted for his services to the sport.

In the mid-1990s, after watching a young Manchester United side lose their opening match of the season 3–1 to Aston Villa, ex-Liverpool star and now TV pundit Alan Hansen remarked: 'You'll win nothing with kids.' The Reds went on to finish the season as Champions, edging ahead of Newcastle for the

League title on the final day of the season, before going on to claim the FA Cup with a 1–0 victory over Liverpool.

The great Charlie Chaplin believed that live theatre would always be more popular than filmed performances. 'The cinema is little more than a fad,' he said in 1916. 'It's a canned drama. What audiences really want is to see flesh and blood on the stage.'

The director Howard Hughes rather failed to predict the success of two great Hollywood careers. He once dismissed James Cagney as a 'little runt'. And another actor was described thus: 'His ears make him look like a taxi-cab with both doors open.' His name? Clark Gable.

The Beatles are still the biggest band there's been in pop music, though their success seemed by no means guaranteed to everyone. When manager Brian Epstein tried to interest the giant record label Decca in the band, he got the terse reply: 'Go back to Liverpool, Mr Epstein. Four-groups are out.'

Fellow musician Henry Mancini meanwhile suggested that the Beatles 'will never last'. And after rowing with John Lennon, the group's original manager Allan Williams claimed: 'You'll never work again.'

Ed Wynn once turned down the chance to play a wizard in a new film, saying the part was too small for him. The movie was *The Wizard of Oz*.

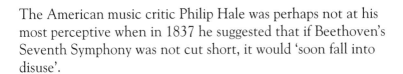

The American music critic Philip Hale was perhaps not at his most perceptive when in 1837 he suggested that if Beethoven's Seventh Symphony was not cut short, it would 'soon fall into disuse'.

The death of the cinema has long been predicted. Writing in the *New Scientist* in 1964, Sir Herbert Read said cinemas would 'disappear by 1984'.

With marvellous understatement – or was it just plain lack of judgement – a talent scout described Fred Astaire after his first audition thus: 'Can't act, can't sing, slightly bald. Can dance a little.'

The BBC shunned a series of pop shows in 1960, with a spokesman for the corporation suggesting: 'The teenage vogue for beat music and rock 'n' roll is over.'

The whole of England was expectant when cricket captain Tony Greig suggested that his team could make the West Indies 'grovel' in the forthcoming Test series in 1976. Unfortunately for him, it was Greig who ended up doing the grovelling as the Caribbean team and its battery of fast bowlers thrashed England 3–0.

The brilliant young actor James Dean recorded a public service advert in 1955 where he stated: 'Take it easy driving. The life you save may be mine.' Two weeks later the young star was killed while speeding in his Porsche car.

❖

Athletics coach Tom McNab told his young charge Daley Thompson that he was a poor runner who would never make it big as a decathlete. Six years later, in 1980, Thompson won the first of his two Olympic gold medals – in the decathlon. He also broke the world record four times.

❖

The first feature film produced by Walt Disney was so expensive to make that experts predicted it would be his last, and described it as 'Disney's folly'. Despite these grim forecasts, *Snow White and the Seven Dwarfs* became one of the most popular children's films of all time.

❖

It's quite unusual for experts to see the result and consequence of their prediction quite as starkly as BBC radio commentator Lieutenant-Commander Tommy Woodroffe in 1938. Describing that year's FA Cup Final, Woodroffe said: 'If there's a goal now, I'll eat my hat.' Sadly for him and his hat there was a score – and the offending item was duly consumed.

❖

Writing in the *Mail on Sunday* in 1997, Victoria Newton foresaw a difficult future for a new movie. 'Director James Cameron's *Titanic* is the latest of seventeen [films about the ship], almost all of which have flopped. That may well be a foretaste of what is to come for the film,' she warned. A few weeks later the film critic of *Time* magazine Richard Corliss said of the film: 'The regretful verdict here is: Dead in the Water.'

Cameron's film went on to become the first to gross more than one billion dollars and won eleven Oscars.

The producers of *Dr No*, the first of the James Bond films, had a number of preferences for the actor to play 007. These included Rex Harrison, David Niven and Cary Grant. The young Scottish actor put forward for the role they initially dismissed as unsuitable to play the suave spy. 'He looks like a bricklayer,' they complained. His name? Sean Connery, the first, and some would say the best, screen Bond.

The head of MGM Louis B. Mayer dismissed the idea that a little rodent could ever make it as a popular cartoon character. 'Every woman is frightened of a mouse,' said Mayer in 1926, failing to foresee the huge success of Mickey Mouse.

As Scotland prepared to play England at Murrayfield in the 1999 Five Nations, one seasoned Scottish rugby commentator said: 'Bookmakers have correctly installed England as 1–14 favourites. We've been asked to remember Jean Van De Velde on Carnoustie's 18th hole, about Celtic and the team with the extremely long name, yet still we cannot give the Scots a prayer.'

The result after that was never in doubt. Scotland won 19–13, robbing England of the Grand Slam for the second year in a row.

Before the 1992 European Championships, England football manager Graham Taylor told the nation's fans: 'Sit back and let me do all the worrying.' What followed was one of the worst

England campaigns ever. Taylor's team struggled to achieve goalless draws against both Denmark and France, before finally going down 2–1 to Sweden.

# Commercial Suicide

*President Bill Clinton's famous campaign theme was 'It's the economy, stupid'. Unfortunately for many experts in finance, economics and trade, that's just what some of their predictions have turned out to be – stupid. Economics, of course, is not an exact science, though that seems little excuse for some of the more outrageous pronouncements some economists have made. Nor are there are excuses for certain business people and politicians who really should have known better when it came to looking ahead at our future wealth and prosperity. After all, they're the experts. Aren't they?*

When in 1859 Edwin L. Drake tried to get drillers involved in his exciting new venture their reaction was simple: 'Drill for oil? You mean drill into the ground to try and find oil? You're crazy.'

Later that year Drake struck oil near Titusville, Pennsylvania, and a new industry was born.

Lyndon B. Johnson, who became US President after the assassination of J. F. K., was in bullish mood in 1965 when he announced: 'So here is the Great Society. It's the time – and it's going to be soon – when nobody in this country is poor.'

The Republican President Herbert Hoover was convinced that the United States was on the threshold of something momentous in 1928. 'We in America today are nearer the final triumph over poverty than ever before in the history of the land,' he claimed. Well, something momentous did occur shortly afterwards – the Wall Street crash of 1929, the prelude to the Great Depression which lasted until the Second World War.

Mind you, Hoover had been in distinguished economic company. No less an authority than Irving Fisher, an economics professor at Yale University, stated not long before the crash: 'Stocks have reached what looks like a permanently high plateau.'

Meanwhile financier Bernard Baruch wrote in June 1929 that: 'The economic condition of the world seems on the verge of a great forward movement.'

Even after the crash occurred, on Thursday 2 October 1929, certain experts were convinced it was a short-lived phenomenon. The day after, J. J. Bernet, President of the Chesapeake and Ohio Railway, said simply: 'I see no cause for alarm.' The US Labour Department happily forecast that 1930 would be a 'splendid employment year' and Irving Fisher, still undaunted, said: 'In the immediate future, the outlook is bright.'

As late as 1931 the lauded financier and banker J. P. Morgan said loftily: 'I don't know anything about any depression.'

Then America woke up to the fact that the Depression was real, ditched Hoover and voted in Franklin Delano Roosevelt as their new president.

Perhaps inevitably, once the Depression was over, and the Second World War was in progress American experts went to the other extreme and warned of the grim future ahead. Academic Dr Hans Elias warned in 1942: 'There will be no cars, radios, washing machines or refrigerators after the war. The post-war world will be so poor that women will have to return to their grand-mother's spinning wheel and men will have to build their own cottages.' By 1945, the Secretary of Commerce Henry A. Wallace warned that unless drastic actions were taken the country would have eight million unemployed and be on the verge of another 'deep depression'.

From 1945 to 1950 the US economy grew by almost half and unemployment barely touched four million.

A research centre in Denmark proudly announced in 1978 that it had managed the world's first viable cross between a potato and a tomato. The 'pomato', as it was inevitably called, was greeted with much excitement as a great way to feed the world. A spokesman for the centre said: 'We look upon the pomato as a major contribution to solving the world's food/population balance...the fruit will combine the taste of the tomato with the nourishing power of the potato.'

It all seemed too good to be true. And it was. Upon further testing, the pomato was also discovered to be poisonous.

Advertising may seem a relatively modern phenomenon, but as with most things on earth, it has a very long history. Indeed as long ago as 1759 *The Idler* magazine was of the following view: 'The trade of Advertising is now so near to perfection that it is not easy to propose any improvements.' Which may come as news to anyone who has had to sit through endless television commercials for soap powders and hair products.

An infamous advert ran in the early 1960s in Britain. It read: 'Distival can be given with complete safety to pregnant women and nursing mothers without adverse effect on mother or child.' Another name for that drug is thalidomide.

An American businessman Malcolm Bricklin somehow persuaded the Government of New Brunswick in Canada to fork out $20 million to fund his revolutionary design for a sports car in 1974. The ground-breaking Bricklin was heralded as the ultimate in sleekness and refinement, and the marketing hype declared: 'It might prove to be the first great sexual experience of your lifetime.' Unfortunately the car, personally backed by the New Brunswick prime minister, ran into a few technical difficulties. The doors wouldn't work, bits fell off when the car moved, and the shock absorbers detached themselves at speeds of more than 35 mph. Customers were also advised not to drive the car in the rain. The economics weren't great either, the cars costing about a thousand dollars more to make than they were being sold for.

Looking ahead to the coming decade, leading businessman Leonard Macham wrote in *The Times* in 1969: 'The 1970s, barring any major set-to between the major powers, show a steady increase in our national prosperity.' By the end of that decade Britain had become known, in economic terms, as the 'Sick Man of Europe'.

Economists can be prone to making outlandish comments. Back in 1959 the Managing Director of the International Monetary Fund stated: 'In all likelihood, world inflation is over.'

When President Franklin D. Roosevelt announced in 1933 that America was abandoning the gold standard – where the currency is linked to the value of gold – the US Budget Director Lewis Douglas told a colleague: 'This is the end of Western civilisation.'

Newspapers have long had a bad reputation for occasional inaccuracy or even skewing of the truth. But the American statesman Thomas Jefferson (1743–1826) thought differently about adverts. 'Advertisements contain the only truths to be relied on in a newspaper,' he loftily declared.

Business people have a certain way with words. Consider the comment of Lord Stokes, Chairman of British Leyland, the car manufacturer, who in 1974 said: 'This company is not bust. We are merely in a cyclical decline.'

Back in August 1968, *Business Week* magazine predicted: 'With over 50 foreign cars already on sale here, the Japanese auto industry isn't likely to carve out a big slice of the US market.'

Japanese cars now make up around one quarter of the entire US market.

In his fascinating book of 1905, *A Hundred Years Hence*, author T. Baron Russell thought he saw a great new future for advertising, thanks to what he regarded as the 'new growth of public intelligence'. He wrote: 'Cheap attention-calling tricks and clap-trap will be wholly replaced, as they are already being greatly replaced, by serious expositions; and advertisements, instead of being mere repetitions of stale catch-words, will be made interesting and informative, so that they will be welcomed instead of being shunned.' Quite so.

Russell also had an interesting view on how everyday commerce would be carried out in the future. 'No doubt the soil of every civilised country will be permeated by vast networks of pneumatic tubes: and all letters and parcels will be thus distributed at a speed hardly credible today.'

Ever the optimist, Russell even had a hopeful view of how trade and business would be practised in the early twenty-first century. He stated: 'What will happen in a hundred years hence is that trade disputes will have disappeared because all the workers will be practically their own employers...the workers in every industry being paid not by fixed wages, but by a share in the produce of their labour.'

When Debbi Fields first suggested her new brand of cookies she was laughed at and told: 'Market research reports say America likes crispy cookies, not soft and chewy cookies like you make.'

Mrs Fields Cookies are now one of the most recognisable brands in the United States.

The Democrat Presidential hopeful, Michael Dukakis, was absolutely certain that steps could be taken to reduce America's crippling budget deficit...he just wasn't sure how many steps it would take. In April 1987 he stated: 'There are only two ways to reduce the budget deficit...We must do both.' By September the solutions seem to have grown. 'There are only three ways to reduce the deficit,' said Mr Dukakis. 'We must do all three.'

Yet by August 1988, Mr Dukakis's options seem to have grown again when he said: 'There are only four ways to reduce the federal budget deficit...we must do all four.'

Perhaps it's just as well he didn't get elected, otherwise that list of solutions might have spiralled out of control...

Big computer firm Hewlett Packard thought they knew what they were doing when they turned down Steve Jobs for a job at the company. 'We don't need you. You haven't got through college yet,' they said. Jobs made other plans – and together with Steve Wozniak founded Apple Computers in 1976.

The British Overseas Airways Corporation (BOAC) thought it had a publicity coup on its hands in 1965 when it heard that a house martin named Bonzo had failed in its annual migration to Nigeria with the rest of the flock. The airline promptly declared that it would step in and fly the little bird to its destination. All went well until Bonzo arrived at Heathrow Airport for the scheduled flight, and was released from his cage to give the awaiting media some action photographs. The aptly-named Bonzo then flew straight out of its cage into a nearby plate-glass window, breaking the poor creature's neck.

The British writer G. K. Chesterton (1874–1936), the author of the Father Brown detective stories, saw little future for advertisements in his 1922 book *What I Saw in America*. Either that or he had a very low view of society. He suggested: 'Peasants and priests and all sorts of practical and sensible people are coming back into power. They will not be affected by advertisements, any more than the priests and peasants of the Middle Ages would have been affected by advertisements. Only a very soft-headed, sentimental and rather servile generation could possibly be affected by advertisements at all.' Ouch.

The financial analyst Joseph Granville boldly boasted in the Spring of 1981: 'I'll never make a serious mistake in the market again.'

By the end of 1983 the Dow Jones index in America stood at around 1258 – more than twice the level that Granville had predicted.

The British popular science writer J. B. S. Haldane gazed into his crystal ball in 1927 and thought he saw an answer to all of our prayers. 'It can be predicted with all security,' said the acclaimed author, 'that in 50 years light will cost one fiftieth of its present price and in all the big cities there will be no such thing as night.'

The journalist and anthropologist John Langdon-Davies, in his ground-breaking 1936 book *A Short History of the Future*, was convinced that energy prices in the future – i.e. now – would be so low that no one could make any money out of it. He predicted: 'Among the many who are doomed to destruction by the march of events, none are more destined to unemployment than the owners, shareholders and directors of our curiously-named Public Utility companies.'

Twenty years later, in 1956, two other 'experts' came to similar conclusions. The founder of *Time* magazine, Henry Luce, stated: 'By 1980 all power – electric, atomic, solar – is likely to be virtually costless.'

And the US scientist John von Neumann suggested: 'A few decades hence, energy may be free – just like the un-metered air.'

All of which may come as something of a surprise to anyone who lived through the oil price crisis of the 1970s caused by an oil boycott led by the Arab nations, or who is now facing increasing petrol, gas and electricity bills.

During the peak of the oil crisis in 1973 the US President Richard Nixon predicted that by the end of that decade America would be self-sufficient in energy and would 'not need to rely on foreign energy'.

In fact, by 1980, the US still depended on foreign oil for more than one third of its consumption.

❖

The British Chancellor of the Exchequer and later Prime Minister Benjamin Disraeli had little doubt that plans for a canal from Port Said to Suez in the Middle East were a waste of time and would never work. 'A most futile attempt and totally impossible to be carried out,' he told MPs in 1858.

The now defunct *Globe* newspaper in London had a similar message in 1859 when it warned: 'No one will ever collect a farthing in tolls from this impossible canal.'

In November 1869 the engineer behind the scheme, Ferdinand de Lesseps, was on board the yacht that became the first vessel to make its way through the new 100-mile-long Suez Canal.

❖

The experts also knew better when it came to the Panama Canal. King Philip II of Spain not only declared in the middle of the sixteenth century: 'If God had wanted a Panama canal, he would have put one here.' He even made it an offence punishable by death to try to build one. Surveyor John C. Trautwine who explored a projected route in 1854 said: 'I cannot entertain the slightest hope that a ship canal will ever be found practicable across any part of it.'

In 1891 the *Scientific American* magazine declared that the whole idea of such a canal linking the Atlantic and the Pacific was a 'thing of the past'.

By 1914, thanks to French and then American engineers, the much-derided canal was open to shipping.

The social commentator John P. Lockhart-Mummery considered in 1936 that tidal power would be a good source of energy for the future. A sensible and far-sighted suggestion, one might think. But then, he did have his own fears about the impact of using too much tidal power. He stated: 'If extensively exploited over a long period of time, however, it might result in bringing the moon too close to the earth for safety.'

Perhaps he was not such a brilliant thinker, then.

Alex Lewyt, who was head of the Lewyt Corporation, a leading maker of vacuum cleaners, was convinced in 1955 that his products had a great future in using alternative sources of energy. He suggested: 'Nuclear powered vacuum cleaners will probably be a reality within ten years.'

A year earlier the Chairman of the Board of the Radio Corporation of America, David Sarnoff, had similar views on the commercial use of nuclear fuels. He said: 'It can be taken for granted that before 1980 ships, locomotives and even automobiles will be atomically fuelled.'

The former Chairman of the Atomic Energy Commission in the US, Dixy Lee Ray, was convinced in 1977 that nuclear energy was not as dangerous as people feared. He stated: 'A nuclear power plant is infinitely safer than eating, because 300 people choke to death on food every year.'

There were fears that the much-vaunted Millennium or Y2K Computer Bug would wreak havoc on businesses world-wide and even bring civilisation as we knew it to a halt. Some estimates claim that as much as £200 billion was spent around the globe trying to prevent disaster occurring. In fact, as the dawn of the new millennium came and went, there were remarkably few mishaps at all. Except for one man. Alonzo Anderson, from Michigan in the US, was injured when propane gas cylinders in his cellar exploded. A sheepish Anderson told the fire fighters who dealt with the blast that he was so afraid of what might happen on 1 January 2000 that he had hoarded large amounts of food, water and other supplies in the basement – including the propane gas which exploded.

# Military Might

*In no other area of life do blunders matter more than in warfare. Make one mistake or poor prediction, and you don't just endanger your own life, but those of many others around you as well. Which helps to explain why some of the more absurd proclamations from our military leaders have made such chilling – as well as grimly amusing – reading down the years. It's also true that military personnel have not always been noted for their imagination or flexibility of thought as much as for their courage and dedication to service. The British Army, for example, was once famously described as composed of 'lions led by donkeys'. Let the braying begin.*

A clue as to why the Roman Empire did not survive militarily might lie in a certain rigidity of thought. By the first century AD the chief military adviser to the emperor, someone called Julius Frontinus, felt sufficiently secure in the Roman machine to stop any more innovations. He announced: 'I will ignore all ideas for new works and engines of war, the invention of which has reached its limits and for whose improvement I see no further hope.'

The great writer and thinker H. G. Wells asserted in 1914 that the Great War, as it was then known, would be not only the greatest of all wars but the last. Sadly, it was not to be and it is now known as the First World War.

'No enemy bomber can reach the Ruhr. If one reaches the Ruhr, my name is not Goering. You may call me Meyer.' So proclaimed Herman Goering, German Air Force Minister, 1939.

During the Second World War Allied bombers penetrated deep into Germany, destroying towns and cities and killing tens of thousands of people.

The head of Britain's armed forces in the First World War, Earl Haig, considered on the eve of war that: 'Bullets have little stopping power against the horse.'

One of his military staff went even further, declaring after a demonstration of the tank: 'The idea that cavalry will be replaced by these iron coaches is absurd. It is little short of treasonous.' Meanwhile the British Secretary of State for War, Lord Kitchener, was simply patronising. 'A pretty mechanical toy,' he sniffed.

This was in fact the war in which the role of the tank decisively replaced the horse in battles. Earl Haig, whose military rank was Field Marshal, didn't have much of a clue about weapons either. Machines guns, he claimed in 1914, were 'grossly overrated' as a weapon. A few years earlier a French General had drawn a similar conclusion about the machine gun. 'Make no mistake,' he told French members of parliament, 'this weapon will change absolutely nothing.'

Hundreds of thousands of soldiers were to die in the ensuing war, mown down by this 'overrated' weapon, effectively making the French and British tactics of massed infantry assaults useless.

At least one man did guess correctly that the coming power of modern weapons would enable humans to kill each other in vastly greater numbers than ever before. However, French physiologist Charles Robert Richet, winner of the Nobel Prize for Medicine in 1913, was not quite so accurate in his assessment of human nature. He declared: 'Quick-firing rifles, monstrous artillery, improved shells, smokeless and noiseless gunpowder – these are so destructive that a great battle could cause the deaths of 300,000 men in a few hours.' Richet continued, optimistically: 'It is evident that the nations, no matter how unconcerned they may be at times when driven by a false pride, will draw back from this fearful vision.'

Even earlier, William E. Lecky (1838–1903) had come up with a similar thought when he suggested: 'Gunpowder and military machinery have rendered the triumph of barbarism impossible. Steam has united nations in the closest bonds.'

Neither Richet's 'fearful vision', nor Lecky's dream of 'united nations' were enough it seems to prevent either world war.

The idea that submarines could have a major role in warfare was ridiculed in the years before the First World War. The writer and futurologist H. G. Wells, for once, failed to see their purpose. 'My imagination refuses to see any sort of submarine doing any more than suffocate its crew and founder at sea,' he wrote in 1902. When another writer Sir Arthur Conan Doyle penned a story called Danger, which warned that Britain could be at risk from a sustained naval blockade by submarines, the very idea was laughed out of the Admiralty.

The British admiral Sir Compton Dombile stated: 'Most improbable, and more like one of Jules Verne's stories.'

The British Admiral Charles Penrose-Fitzgerald stated in 1914: 'I do not think that any civilised nation will torpedo unarmed and defenceless merchant ships.' On 7 May 1915, a German U-boat U-20 torpedoed the unarmed RMS *Lusitania*, which sank in just eighteen minutes. In all 1,201 men, women and children died, including three German prisoners in the merchant ship's cells.

By then Germany had already announced a submarine blockade of the British Isles.

Jules Verne (1828–1905) the great French science fiction writer, and author of *Twenty Thousand Leagues Under the Sea* among other works, had in fact clearly foreseen the military value of submarines. But perhaps he was guilty of a little overenthusiasm when he suggested in 1904: 'The submarine may be the cause of bringing battle to a stoppage altogether, for fleets will become useless, and as other war machinery continues to improve, war will become impossible.'

The advent of the Second World War, so clear in hindsight, baffled many so-called experts at the time. In May 1938 the *Daily Express* announced that there would be no major European war in 'this year or the next'. More famously in September 1938, the then British Prime Minister Neville Chamberlain returned from a 'peace' conference with Hitler in Munich waving a piece of paper and declaring: 'My good friends, for the second time in our history, a British Prime Minister has returned from Germany bringing peace with honour. I believe it is "peace for our time". Go home and get a nice quiet sleep.'

Within a year, in September 1939, the Second World War had begun.

The US President, Franklin D. Roosevelt, was anxious to dispel the claims of his fellow countrymen who feared that America would get drawn into the 'European' war that began in 1939. Addressing an election rally in 1940 F. D. R. declared: 'I have told you once and I tell you again – your boys will not be sent into any foreign wars.' This of course was before the Japanese attacked Pearl Harbour less than two years later and before F. D. R. sent hundreds of thousands of American 'boys' to start the re-invasion of mainland Europe in June 1944.

The Earl of Birkenhead was unhappy in 1930 that the League of Nations – the now defunct forerunner to the United Nations – had prohibited the use of gas in warfare. Surely, his Lordship argued in *The World in 2030*, scientists could soon come up with gases which would cause 'prolonged insensibility' yet no serious after-effects. 'The introduction of such gases,'

Birkenhead concluded, 'would obviously revolutionize warfare. It might conceivably make battles, as we understand them, impossible.'

One of Lord Birkenhead's other great predictions was what he described as the 'perfect war-machine' which would be part tank, part ship, part aeroplane and part submarine and capable of fighting on the land, in the air, and under and on top of the water. 'Though many will deride this conception as fantastic,' he conceded, 'its attainment is certainly not to be lightly dismissed.'

After the French had surrendered to the Germans in June 1940, following a brief but stunning invasion, at least one French military leader predicted that Britain would be the next to fall. General Maxime Weygand said: 'In three weeks England will have her neck wrung like a chicken.'

As Winston Churchill later commented, 'Some neck, some chicken'.

A book was published in France in 1939 with the fascinating title *Is an Invasion Still Possible?* This referred to the age-old French fear that France was vulnerable to attack from German invasion, as had been the case in earlier wars. The book concluded that France was in fact no longer at risk from such an attack. In a notable introduction to the book, Marshall Henri Petain poured scorn on the idea that German tanks in particular could menace the French border. 'As for tanks,' he wrote, 'which are supposed by some to bring us a shortening of wars, their incapacity is striking.'

A year later, the German military stormed into France, conquering the country in two months in one of the most rapid invasions in the history of warfare. Among the key elements to this blitzkrieg attack were the power and speed of the German tank divisions.

Petain himself became the nominal head of the Vichy Government in France, which collaborated with the invading Nazis during the Second World War.

Towards the end of the sixteenth century, as the tactics of warfare were changing, there were still strong voices against ditching the time-honoured weapons of bow and arrow or crossbow in favour of newer means of attack. Colonel Sir John Smyth told the Privy Council in England: 'The bow is a simple weapon, firearms are very complicated things which get out of order in many ways.'

The Nobel Prizes, including those for peace, are named after Alfred Bernhard Nobel (1833–1896) who invented dynamite in 1867 and gelignite in 1875. The chemist and engineer was convinced, however, that his discoveries would lead to less, not more destruction. He said: 'My dynamite will sooner lead to peace than a thousand world conventions. As soon as men will find that in one instant whole armies can be utterly destroyed, they surely will abide by golden peace.'

A spokesman for the Vichy Government in France, which collaborated with the Nazi regime during the 1939–45 war, used to end his news bulletins with the words: 'Like Carthage, England will be destroyed.'

The horrors of warfare are often underestimated by each succeeding generation. The eminent British scientist and author J. B. S. Haldane optimistically suggested in 1937: 'I do not believe in the possibility of anything much worse than mustard gas being produced.'

The nineteenth-century French statesman and scientist François Arago was dismissive about the value of a new invention, the railways, in helping his country's war effort. In words that may have made Napoleon himself proud, he stated in 1836: 'Transport by railroad car would result in the emasculation of our troops and would deprive them of the option of the great marches which have played such an important role in the triumph of our armies.'

Arago's great insight into military logistics was rewarded in 1848 with his appointment as Minister of War.

Understatement was not something normally associated with General George Custer of the US cavalry. But as Custer looked down at the Sioux Indian encampment in June 1876 he turned to his 700 men and yelled: 'Hold your horses boys. There's plenty down there for all of us.'

Custer certainly had an unfortunate way with words. Years earlier he had claimed: 'The Army is the Indian's best friend.'

The US Secretary of the Navy in 1922 confidently asserted that no one could make an unexpected attack on any of their positions in the Pacific. After all, he said: 'Radio makes surprise impossible.' Alas, no one told the Japanese that, and even though radio technology had improved by December 1941, the Japanese were still able to launch a devastating – and surprise – attack on the US base at Pearl Harbor in Hawaii.

John Langdon-Davies, in his book *A Short History of the Future*, wrote in 1935: 'There will be no war in western Europe for the next five years.'

The American astronomer William Henry Pickering was just one of a number of 'experts' who saw little military value in the use of aircraft. In 1908 he observed: 'A popular fallacy is to suppose that flying machines could be used to drop dynamite on an enemy in time of war.' Another who doubted the role of aeroplanes was Marshal Ferdinand Foch, a leading French military figure who said in 1911 that flying machines were 'interesting toys but of no military value'.

Even after a war has begun, there has often been unfounded optimism that it would end soon and stop other conflicts. Many voices in 1914 suggested that the European war which had just started would be over 'by Christmas'. In fact it was not until 1918, and after ten million lives were lost, that the conflict stopped.

US President Richard Nixon was also optimistic in 1971 when he was talking about the Vietnam War. 'I seriously doubt if we will have another war. This is probably the last.'

Even after the First World War, where planes had played a role, military strategists were unconvinced that aircraft could make much difference. The US Secretary of War in 1921, John Wingate Weeks, pointed out that General John Pershing, the head of the US forces in the First World War, hadn't even looked into an aeroplane, never mind gone up in one. 'If they had been of such importance he'd have tried at least one ride,' said Weeks. 'We'll stick to the army on the ground and the battleships at sea.'

As the Second World War approached, such attitudes stayed unchanged. One commentator, Arlington B. Conway, suggested: 'Air forces by themselves will never do to great cities what Rome did to Carthage or what the Assyrians did to Jerusalem.' While in 1937, US Colonel John W. Thomason said: 'It is not possible to concentrate enough military planes with military loads over a modern city to destroy that city.'

Within a few years, during World War Two, cities such as London, Coventry, Hamburg and Dresden suffered massive destruction at the hands of sustained bombing campaigns.

The year was 1904 and the Russians were feeling bitter at their recent defeat by Japanese troops in the Far East. Smarting at this reversal, Tsar Nicholas II gave orders for his Baltic Fleet to make the arduous journey to teach the Japanese a lesson at sea. The fleet set sail under the command of Admiral Rozhestrensky, who settled down for the voyage ahead. After just two days, however, the Admiral was wakened from his slumber by a nervous subordinate with the news that the fleet was under imminent danger of attack from hostile forces. Rozhestrensky immediately gave the order to attack and soon the ships' guns were booming away. After some time however the Admiral's men became suspicious that no one was returning the fire. Upon further inspection, they discovered the reason why. The Russian Fleet was still in the North Sea near the Dogger Bank, some seventy miles off the English coast. And what they had thought was a surprise Japanese fleet in disguise was in fact a flotilla of harmless fishing trawlers out of Hull which had until then been peacefully plying their trade.

One trawler had been sunk in the attack, two fishermen killed and six injured.

This turned out to be the only success for Admiral Rozhestrensky and his men. When, after five months, they eventually reached the Sea of Japan in May 1905 they were quickly routed by the waiting Japanese Navy.

When, in 1921, an American officer, Brigadier General Billy Mitchell, claimed that the use of aircraft against battleships could be crucial in future wars, he was treated with contempt. The US Secretary of the Navy Josephus Daniels snorted: 'Good God! This man should be writing dime novels!' And the US Secretary of War Newton D. Baker said: 'That idea is so damned nonsensical and impossible that I'm willing to stand on the bridge of a battleship while that nitwit tries to hit it from the air.'

Mitchell in fact proved he could hit a ship by later sinking a captured German battleship with aerial bombing during a practice exercise, but the experts still knew better.

The US Assistant Secretary of the Navy, Theodore Roosevelt Jnr, made what he considered an important qualification. 'Such an experiment without actual conditions of war to support it is a foolish waste of time. I once saw a man kill a lion with a 30-30 calibre rifle under certain conditions, but that doesn't mean that a 30-30 rifle is a lion gun.'

This brilliant reasoning continued right up to November 1941 when the US Navy claimed: 'It is significant that despite the claims of air enthusiasts no battleship has yet been sunk by bombs.'

The following month Japanese aircraft destroyed much of the US Pacific Fleet and sank two of the Royal Navy's most powerful battleships: *The Prince of Wales* and *Repulse*.

Timing is everything when it comes to the very best predictions. Wendell Wilkie, who had been comfortably defeated in the US Presidential election the year before, was at dinner on 7 December 1941, when a fellow guest ventured to suggest that America would be at war with Japan within forty-eight hours. Wilkie was adamant. 'We won't be at war with Japan within forty-eight hours, within forty-eight days, within forty-eight years,' he insisted. Seconds later the phone rang. The news was grim. Japanese planes had just bombed Pearl Harbor.

Not everyone involved in the atomic bomb project in the US in 1945 thought it had any chance of working. An adviser to President Harry Truman, Admiral William Daniel Leahy, was quite insistent. 'This is the biggest fool thing we have ever done. The bomb will never go off – and I speak as an expert in explosives!'

Later that year the US dropped the first of two nuclear bombs on mainland Japan, killing tens of thousands and hastening the end of World War Two in the Pacific.

The British wartime leader, Winston Churchill, was another who did not fully appreciate the dangerous potential of the nuclear bomb. In 1939 he mused: 'Atomic energy might be as good as our present day explosives but it is unlikely to produce anything very much more dangerous.'

The nuclear arms race began during the Second World War and increased in speed afterwards – a little too quickly for some. The 'authoritative' writer William L. Laurence was confident in 1948 that the Soviet Union was still some way behind America when it came to nuclear weapons. He wrote: 'We still have at least four years as of today before Russia can begin producing A-bombs of her own.' Laurence added: 'It may of course take her much longer, particularly since her scientists – forced to work under the ever-present shadow of possible liquidation – lack the atmosphere of intellectual freedom so vital to creative efficiency.'

In the same year, the military head of the nuclear project in the US, Lieutenant General Leslie R. Groves, stated: 'It will take Russia at least until 1955 to produce atomic bombs in quantity.'

Within a year Russian scientists had not only successfully tested their own nuclear bomb, they had begun the large-scale production of them as weapons.

The hazards of nuclear war have not always been taken as seriously as we take them now. For example, US Colonel Robert Rutherford McCormick was confident that his country at least had little to fear from atomic bombs in 1950 – even if he was a little less confident about the rest of us. 'The dangers of atomic war are overrated,' he announced. 'It would be hard on little, concentrated countries like England. In the United States we have lots of space.' So that's all right, then.

Meanwhile the Deputy Undersecretary for Defence for Research and Engineering, Thomas K. Jones, was even more optimistic about the chances of survival. 'Dig a hole, cover it with a couple of doors and then throw three feet of dirt on top,' he advised. 'It's the dirt that does it. You know, dirt is just great stuff. If there are enough shovels to go around, everybody's going to make it.'

# A Matter of Faith

*Religion and prophecies are fertile terrain for anyone
fascinated by predictions. Religious leaders have always been
prone to make forecasts for the future, though the wiser ones
have always ensured the predicted dates fall well outside their
own lifetimes. Then there are those constant predictions of the
end of the world, which reached yet another peak at the start
of this Millennium. The truth is that some humans have
always liked to make important-sounding prophecies, and
many of the rest of us are only too eager to listen. This is
fine, just as long as we don't take the prophets' words too
seriously or literally.*

Doubtless motivated by noble sentiments, the US National
Society of Christians named Belfast as their 'Model City of the
World' at the end of the 1960s. Their reason: 'Belfast possesses
a zealous Christian attitude and participates with an active
interest in religious functions.'

A sentiment few at the time could deny.

The Beatles singer John Lennon plucked out his crystal ball in
1964 and declared: 'Christianity will go. It will vanish and
shrink. I needn't argue about that – I'm right and will be
proved right.' This was Lennon's prelude to his now infamous
comment: 'We're more popular than Jesus now.'

A former atheist named William Alexander Miller became
convinced by his reading of various books of the Bible –
especially Revelations – that the world was about to end. More
than that, he knew how it was going to happen – consumption
by fire, and when – some time in 1843 or 1844. The Millerite
movement as it was known attracted a great deal of devotees in
the United States – something like a million people all told
may have attended his meetings and he had 100,000 loyal
followers. As the great day approached in 1844 (22 October
was finally chosen after several false alarms) the followers
prepared for the moment of reckoning. The most fanatical
killed their friends and family before killing themselves,
sensibly believing that the dead would get to God first. Others
lay down waiting in newly dug mass graves or waited in
graveyards, and many wore expensive 'ascension robes' which
Miller had thoughtfully sold them so they could look their best
for the great occasion. What a shame, then, that 22 October

came and went and New England, and indeed the rest of the world, carried on pretty much as before. Except of course for the 100,000 Millerites who left their prophet's side, disillusioned but maybe just a little bit wiser.

Sometimes a prophet needs a bit of luck, and that's what happened with the sixteenth-century German astrologer and man of mystery Johannes Stoeffler. He caused a bit of a stir by announcing that the world would end in a giant flood on 20 February 1524. With the stories of Noah firmly in their mind, many credulous peasants dashed off makeshift boats – or arks if you will – to float on the River Rhine to prepare for the coming of the waters. Now maybe Stoeffler was just lucky, or maybe a gifted weather forecaster, but when the day came storms and rains did indeed cause widespread havoc. Unfortunately for those in little craft the stormy weather was very dangerous. Many of the boats capsized and their occupants died – a fate which was unlikely to have befallen them had they stayed on land. Another victim was Count von Iggleheim who, upon hearing of Stoeffler's doom-laden prediction, had a three-level ark built in preparation for the floods. Alas for Iggleheim the idea proved a little too popular and the poor man was trampled to death by people trying to clamber on board his ship.

Over in London a group of astrologers had also decided that a great flood would come and sweep the city away, with this one predicted for 1 February 1524. At least 20,000 fled to the tops of hills to escape the expected torrents and one churchman even stocked up two months' worth of supplies inside a specially built fortress. When the date failed to produce any more rain than you'd expect in February in London, the astrologers cannily got together and discovered that owing to a small mistake, they'd actually meant 1624, not 1524 – conveniently far in the future.

An expert on exorcism, Canon John Pearce-Higgins got himself in something of a linguistic muddle when he stated in 1973: 'Sometimes I have a devil of a job convincing ghosts they are actually dead.'

In his work *The Rotarian*, Stewart C. McFarland made it clear that he thought the members of the Rotary Club and similar organisations were made of the finer stuff. He wrote in the 1924 book: 'Had an Optimist, Co-operative, Exchange, Kiwanis, Lions or a Rotary Club flourished in the days of the Exodus, with Moses as president, the children of Israel would have reached the promised land in forty days instead of forty years.'

Benito Mussolini, apart from being fat and a dictator, was a home-spun philosopher too – just not a very good one. In the 1930s he declared: 'Fascism is a religion; the twentieth century will be known in history as the century of Fascism.'

One of the great wonders of the Universe are the comets that flit around our solar system and beyond; or at least that's how we like to see them. For the Catholic scholar, Father Augustion de Angelis, writing in 1673, they were nowhere near as remote. 'Comets are not heavenly bodies,' he reasoned, 'but originate in the earth's atmosphere below the moon; for everything heavenly is eternal and incorruptible, but comets have a beginning and ending – ergo, comets cannot be heavenly bodies.'

❖

When two small earthquakes hit London in 1761, one on
8 February, the next on 8 March, one William Bell was
convinced that they heralded the end of the world. The
earthquakes had been twenty-eight days apart, and so Bell
predicted that the next one would be on 5 April and would
flatten the city. His followers took to the Thames or made for
the hills to escape the carnage, but the date passed by
uneventfully. Bell was thrown into a lunatic asylum for his
troubles.

❖

The sixteenth-century German religious reformer Martin
Luther, the father of the modern Protestant Church, was very
much a creature of his time. He bitterly criticised his
contemporary, Polish astronomer and scientist Copernicus.
'People give ear to an upstart astrologer (*sic*) who strove to
show that the earth revolves – not the heavens, or the
firmament, the sun and the moon. This fool wishes to reverse
the entire science of astronomy; but sacred Scripture tells us
that Joshua commanded the sun to stand still and not the
earth.'

❖

On the other side of the Christian divide, a Jesuit called Father
Melchior Inchofer was just as emphatic on the subject in 1632:
'The opinion of the earth's motion is of all the heresies the
most abominable, the most pernicious, the most scandalous;
the immovability of the earth is thrice sacred; argument against
the immortality of the soul, the existence of God, and the
Incarnation, should be tolerated sooner than an argument to
prove that the earth moves.'

The scientist Sir Richard Proctor was pessimistic about the chances of humankind surviving cosmological collisions. In early 1897 he warned: 'In about 1897–1898 the sun will be so enormously increased by the impact of a comet as to destroy life upon this earth.'

Perhaps mindful of the cricket-mad Australian public, the Revd T. McVittie, a churchman in Sydney, made a startling suggestion in 1937. 'If Christ came to Sydney today,' said the Revd McVittie, 'he would be on "the Hill" [a popular and traditionally rowdy part of the Sydney ground] at cricket matches driving home the lessons of the game. One can imagine Christ reminding the crowd that Satan was the deadliest and most determined googly bowler of all time.'

The Great Pyramid of Cheops proved an inspiration for those looking for the end of the world. After experts had measured its dimensions, they declared that the world would end in 1881. This was later upgraded to 1936, and then 1953, after which damp squib people began to lose faith in the structure's predictive powers. The Scottish astronomer Charles Piazzi Smyth was similarly smitten by the dimensions of the Great Pyramid, which he believed indicated that Judgement Day would arrive somewhere between 1892 and 1911. Despite leaving his prediction quite wide, Smyth was to be disappointed.

Chilean astronomer Munoz Ferradas underlined the dangers of prophecies when he suggested that all life on this planet would be destroyed by a comet hitting the earth in August 1944. The prediction led to a number of suicides by panicky Chileans, while many more fled into the Andes to escape the impact, and refused to come back for weeks.

❖

The deeply religious and wonderfully-named Cyrus Reed Teed was convinced that the planet was not quite as we know it – and in fact curved the other way. He said in 1889: 'To know of the earth's concavity is to know God, while to believe in the earth's convexity is to deny Him and all His works.'

❖

The American ambassador to the UN, Andrew Young, was in optimistic mood after the 1979 revolution in Iran, in which the Shah was overthrown by religious opposition. He said: 'One day Ayatollah Khomeini will be viewed as some kind of saint.' As recently as 1978, the Shah of Iran had felt sufficiently secure to declare: 'No one can overthrow me.'

And in January 1979, the Shah said: 'I should like very much to take a vacation.' It turned out to be a little more drastic and longer than he might have hoped.

❖

During the hostage crisis in Iran in 1979, Pope John Paul II appealed in the name of Christian principles for the release of those held captive at the US Embassy in the capital Tehran. The new leader of Iran, Ayatollah Khomeini, responded by referring to the actions of the US President Jimmy Carter. 'If Jesus Christ were alive today,' declared the Ayatollah, 'he would impeach Carter.'

❖

The leader of the Japanese group Aum Shinrikyo, the Master Shoko Asahara, declared in 1992 that he knew when the final days of the world would arrive. 'Armageddon will occur at the end of this century,' said the Master. 'Only a race of compassionate sages will survive. Their leader will come from Japan.' In 1994, members of this so-called 'doomsday cult' began a terror campaign in Japan, culminating in an attack on the Tokyo subway with the deadly nerve agent sarin in March 1995, which left twelve people dead.

The colourful Hector Cox was a familiar figure in London where he often gave talks on the Egyptian Book of the Dead. Then, on 27 June 1954, Cox declared that the world would end inside 24 hours. Sadly it was true – at least for Cox. The next day he was found dead, stabbed through the heart. The verdict on his sudden death was suicide.

There is nothing quite so touching – or barmy – as someone who sticks firmly to their views in the face of overwhelming evidence to the contrary. So you have to admire Margaret Missen, who in the 1950s wrote *The Sun Goes Round the Earth*. In it she argues: 'If the Earth did move at tremendous speed, how could we keep a grip on it with our feet? We could walk only very slowly; and should find it slipping rapidly under our footsteps. Then, which way is it running? If we walked in the direction of its tremendous speed, it would push us on terribly rapidly. But if we tried to walk against its revolving…? Either way we should be terribly giddy, and our digestive processes impossible.'

When someone wants to tell another person that they are absolutely certain of a fact they often say: 'Is the Pope a Catholic?' However, according to one Father Charles Coughlin, leader of the Christian Front movement, the answer to that simple and apparently obvious question may be 'no'. He said in 1938: 'The first thirty-three popes were Jews. Among the last ten popes we've had, three were predominantly Jewish.'

There is a certain kind of logic to the argument of Wilbur Glenn Voliva who claimed that the sun was nowhere near the size (865,000 miles in diameter) or the distance from the earth (just under 93 million miles) that scientists suggest. 'The sun is only 32 miles across and no more than 3,000 miles from the earth,' said Wilbur in 1915. 'It stands to reason it must be so. God made the sun to light the earth, and therefore must have placed it close to the task it was designed to do.'

President Jimmy Carter, as he then was, puzzled many when he suggested in 1976: 'I am convinced that UFOs exist because I have seen one.'

The Archbishop of Canterbury Geoffrey Fisher clearly had his doubts about the value of scientific endeavour when he commented in 1950: 'The only thing that science has done for men in the last one hundred years is to create for him fresh moral problems.'

The English churchman Bishop Hugh Latimer had a sure feeling just when the end of the world was coming. Writing in 1552 the Bishop noted: 'The world was ordained to endure, as all learned men affirm, 6,000 years. Now, of that number, there be passed 5,553 years, so that there is no more left than 448.' The Protestant Latimer's own end came rather more abruptly when he was burned at the stake for heresy in 1555 under the reign of the devoutly Catholic Queen Mary.

---

The founder of the Jehovah's Witnesses Charles Taze Russell was quite certain about the timing of the Second Coming. Writing in 1910, in *Studies in Scripture*, he stated confidently: 'The deliverance of the saints must take place some time before 1914.' When 1914 came and passed, and there was still no Second Coming, Russell's followers were unabashed. In the 1923 edition of *Studies in Scripture*, the passage was changed to read: 'The deliverance of the saints must take place some time after 1914.'

---

The congregation at Claymore Memorial Church were just listening to the opening notes of 'Riches Shall Fall From Heaven on High' when there was indeed an almighty crashing from above. A building inspector by the name of David Raiment had been on the roof when it gave way over the heads of the churchgoers.

---

The former NASA space engineer Edgar C. Whisenant wrote a book entitled *88 Reasons Why the Rapture Will Be in 1988*. This book was his explanation of why the 'Rapture' or end of the world would occur then. This led to an End of the World Tour to the Holy Land in 1988 in which an American prophecy teacher, Charles Taylor, promised a grandstand view of the end. He stated: 'We stay at the Intercontinental Hotel right on the Mount of Olives where you can get the beautiful view of the Eastern Gate and the Temple Mount. And if this is the year of our Lord's return, as we anticipate, you may even ascend to glory from within a few feet of His ascension.'

The end didn't occur, and the travellers must have been relieved at least that their tour package price included the return journey 'if necessary'. Whisenant, meanwhile, was forced to write a sequel called *Many Pearls of the End Time*, which suggested a new date for the ultimate end, September 1989. He still didn't get it right.

In 1957, one Mademoiselle Gabrielle Henriet published *Heaven & Earth*, a delightful and deliciously weird critique of travel by aircraft on a rotating earth, an idea she could not quite grasp. She wrote: 'An aircraft flying [at 1,000 kilometres an hour] in the same direction as that of the rotation could not cover any ground at all. It would remain suspended in mid-air above the spot from which it took off, since both speeds are equal. There would, in addition, be no need to fly from one place to another situated on the same latitude. The aircraft could just rise and wait for the desired country to arrive in the ordinary course of the rotation, and then land; although it is difficult to see how any plane could manage to touch ground at all on an airfield which is slipping away at the rate of 1,000 kph. It might certainly be useful to know what people who fly think of the rotation of the earth.' Indeed.

The Pastor of the Lutheran Memorial Church in Madison, Wisconsin, the Revd A. J. Soldan, told his congregation in 1926: 'If the Apostle Paul had been here Saturday, he would have enjoyed seeing the Wisconsin–Iowa football game.'

When asked why he was publishing a magazine such as *Sports Illustrated* in 1960, Henry Luce, the publisher of *Time* magazine, responded: 'I think the world is going to blow up in seven years. The public is entitled to a good time during those seven years.' The world did end in seven years – for Mr Luce, who died in February 1967.

※

The good vicar of Pontesbury, one Reverend Yeomans, answered his own query about the future at a memorable service. His congregation were singing 'I Cannot Help But Wonder Where I'm Bound' and the vicar wanted to inject a little more energy into the proceedings so he began to dance up and down in the aisle. Suddenly the Reverend Yeomans was only too aware where he was bound – the floor had given way and he plunged out of sight into the hot atmosphere of the boiler room below.

※

The world can be a confusing place, or at least that's what the American Ambassador to the United Nations, Warren Austin, may have thought in 1948 when he asked the Jews and Arabs in the Middle East to solve their difficulties 'like good Christians'.

※

A significant number of Christians believed that the Second Coming of Jesus Christ would occur at the time of the new millennium.

For example, a poll for *Time/CNN* in April 1993 found that twenty per cent of Americans agreed that '…the second coming of Jesus Christ will occur sometime around the year 2000'. And in 1999 a poll for *Newsweek* showed that four in ten Americans believed that the world would end with the battle of Armageddon as described in the Bible, and that fifteen per cent thought Jesus would return to earth by the year 2000.

# Our Masters' Voices

*We all like to have a moan at our politicians: how they lie to us, deceive us, and how they never quite manage to do what they promised to do. But perhaps we should be a little more appreciative. After all, don't they give us hours of fun with all the things they say? Where else can you get such a collection of daft, stupid or simply dotty predictions? Where better than in political life to find the truly inspired gaffes and appalling forecasts of our future?*
*Maybe instead of criticising we should just sit back and enjoy the madness.*

At the beginning of May 1902 it was apparent to just about everyone on the Caribbean island of Martinique that the volcano called Mont Pelée was going to erupt very soon. Large holes in the ground were appearing, and boiling mud started to appear. The biggest clue may have been when scores of deadly and aggressive fer-de-lance snakes slithered down the mountain to escape the burning ash and made their way into the nearby capital St Pierre – where they killed at least 50 people. But while evacuation may have seemed the safest option, the island's Governor Louis Mouttet was concerned about the approaching election, and didn't want to lose his control of potential voters. So over the coming days Mouttet organised a campaign in which he sought to reassure the townsfolk that their lives were not in danger. Even as mud slides and falling ash claimed more lives, the Governor announced: 'The safety of St Pierre is absolutely assured.' On 8 May, as the sun came up, the volcano erupted with ferocious force, covering the entire town with deadly hot ash and gases. Out of a population of very nearly 30,000, just two people survived – a shoemaker, and a convict who was in a poorly-ventilated cell and thus safe from toxic gases.

In 1962 the British MP Sir Gerald Nabarro confidently declared that Edward Heath would never become Prime Minister because the public would 'never stomach a bachelor at 10 Downing Street'. That, however, didn't stop the still unmarried Heath becoming Conservative Prime Minister in 1970.

Heath's successor as Conservative leader, Margaret Thatcher, was prone to predictions herself. In 1969, when she was made Shadow Education Spokesman, Thatcher insisted that no woman would become Premier in her political lifetime. In just under ten years she had herself got a new job – as Prime Minister.

Oswald Mosley, the one-time leader of the British fascist movement, said in 1938: 'We shall reach the helm within five years.' By 1940 and the start of war, Mosley had been interned in a camp by the authorities.

Perhaps he was just joking. The poet Hillaire Belloc said in 1921: 'I know of no method by which an aristocratic nation like England can become a democracy.'

Adolf Hitler wasn't just an evil dictator, he was also very bad at predicting the future. Soon after he came to power in Germany in the 1930s he stated: 'By this revolution the German way of life is definitely settled for a thousand years.'

Another offering from the dictator: 'In a hundred years our language (i.e. German) will be the language of Europe.'

Hitler also stated: 'England and America will one day have a war with one another, which will be waged with the greatest hatred imaginable. One of the two countries will have to disappear.'

Meanwhile Aussies might be interested to hear yet another of Hitler's insights into the future: 'The Japanese are occupying all the islands one after another. They will get hold of Australia as well. The White Race will disappear from those regions.'

One of Hitler's most bovine remarks came in 1934, soon after he took power: 'We are winning international respect.'

Perhaps the most absurd of all came in 1941 and during the mass slaughter of millions of Jews: 'Thank God,' said Hitler, 'that I've always avoided persecuting my enemies.'

It's enough to make any newspaper editor wince in sympathy. The *Chicago Daily Tribune* was so certain of the outcome in the 1948 Presidential election that its headline overnight – compiled before the results were actually in – read: 'Dewey Defeats Truman'.

In fact as history records, Harry S. Truman comfortably beat his opponent Thomas E. Dewey by more than two million of the popular vote and by 303 electoral votes to 189. Truman held up the offending headline for what remains a famous political photograph – and constant reminder of the paper's mistake.

The election of John F. Kennedy as US President in 1960 may seem inevitable in hindsight, but many doubted whether the young man would ever be up to the job. When he decided to go for the job, even his father Joseph P. Kennedy remarked: 'He won't have a chance.'

Another famous political family was even less optimistic. Franklin D. Roosevelt Jnr, son of the former president F. D. R., said after meeting Kennedy: 'How can a guy this politically immature seriously expect to be president?' Well he did, and he was, Kennedy beating Republican Richard Nixon in November 1960.

❖

Sometimes people can't help telling us what they really think, especially when they are trying to tell us something completely different. A Conservative woman councillor said in the 1970s: 'Oh yes, we Tory councillors have done a lot for race relations. I do think it's very important.' None of which anyone could object to. But she just couldn't stop herself adding: 'I mean, after all, but for the grace of God, we'd be black ourselves, wouldn't we?'

❖

The Conservative Prime Minister Edward Heath got carried away by uncharacteristic euphoria when he declared in November 1973: 'Our only problem at the moment is the problem of success.' That pronouncement seemed a little hollow just a few months later when his Government fell after a period of industrial unrest and the forced imposition of a three-day working week.

❖

When the little-known Jimmy Carter put himself forward in 1975 to be the Democratic candidate for the 1976 presidential election few people had even heard of him, and fewer still gave him a chance of getting the nomination. In a poll of the influential Democratic National Committee just three per cent thought Carter would get the nod. When against all prediction he got the nomination, many still thought he had no chance in the election itself. Pundit Dick Tuck said Carter 'looks more like a kid in a bus stop with his name pinned on his sweater on his way to summer camp than a President on the way to the White House.'

Carter beat Gerald Ford and made it to Washington.

When Lenin led fellow Marxists in a campaign of 'agitation' in 1905 the Russian police chief Zvolianski was dismissive. 'Nothing will come of them for at least fifty years.' The Russian Revolution began in 1917.

Even when it was well under way, some Russians couldn't bring themselves to admit that the communist system was here to stay for a while. Prince Kropotkin, writing in 1920, said: 'The attempt to build up a communist republic on the lines of strongly centralized state Communism, under the iron rule of the dictatorship of a party, is ending in failure.' It was more than 70 years before the Soviet Union finally began to break up.

The Soviet leader Joseph Stalin provided some unintentional black humour for the Russian people by stating in 1935: 'Gaiety is the most outstanding feature of the Soviet Union.'

The former actor and Governor of California Ronald Reagan was written off when he tried to become the Republican candidate for the 1980 Presidential election. NBC political correspondent Tom Pettit told his viewers: 'I would like to suggest that Ronald Reagan is politically dead.'

Nonetheless this 'dead' political candidate not only won the nomination – he won the White House too and then secured a second term.

Henry Kissinger should have followed his own advice when he spoke about the US Presidential candidate Richard Milhous

Nixon in 1968. 'That man is a disaster,' said Kissinger. 'I would never work for that man.' Not long after Nixon's victory, Kissinger was doing just that.

❖

It seems that Richard 'Tricky Dicky' Nixon was in fact surrounded by people who didn't seem to understand the nature of their man. His Director of Communications said: 'Truth will become the hallmark of the Nixon Administration.' While his Vice President Spiro Agnew said: 'What does a politician have but his credibility?' Some British commentators were equally myopic about Nixon. In 1972, at the Republican's re-election, the pugnacious right-wing writer and political commentator George Gale insisted: 'At worst, Nixon is likely to be the best of a bad lot. At the best he could become the greatest of the post-war presidents.'

Two years later, in August 1974, Nixon became the first and so far only US President to resign, faced with impeachment over the Watergate scandal. Agnew himself had resigned earlier in October 1973 over allegations of financial irregularities.

❖

The great Russian revolutionary Leon Trotsky once declared that 'England is at last ripe for Revolution.' That was in 1925.

❖

The Professor of Moral and Political Philosophy at William and Mary College – the second oldest in America – was certain of one thing in 1917. 'If there is any conclusion in politics on which we can securely rely, both from history and from the laws which govern human action, it is this: that universal suffrage and freedom were and never can be co-existent.'

The suggestion that women should be able to vote was greeted with some dramatic warnings and prophecies in the nineteenth century. The editor of *Harper's* magazine stated in 1853: 'Nothing could be more anti-Biblical than letting women vote.' For *The Catholic World* a decade or so later, allowing women to cast a vote would be nothing less than the end of the 'family union'. Even more was at stake according to the *Eclectic Magazine* in 1874, which warned: 'The love of liberty and the desire of being governed by law alone appears to be characteristically male. If power were put in the hands of the women, free government, and with it liberty of opinion, would fall.'

Former US President Grover Cleveland, who in 1885 became the first Democrat to be elected President after the Civil War, was reassuring on the matter. He said in 1905: 'Sensible and responsible women do not want to vote. The relative positions to be assumed by man and woman in the working out of our civilisation were assigned long ago by a higher intelligence than ours.'

Yet despite all these dire warnings, women were first given the vote in Britain in 1918, and in the United States in 1920.

According to the pundits, Abraham Lincoln had no chance of winning the presidential election of 1864 against his Democrat opponent General George B. McClellan. The editor of the *New York Tribune*, Horace Greely, said on 14 August of that year: 'Mr Lincoln is already beaten. He cannot be re-elected.'

Later that year Lincoln won the election by the huge margin of 212 electoral votes to 21.

❖

Despite his recent ousting as dictator in Cuba by the new kid on the block, Fidel Castro, General Fulgencio Batista was in confident mood in 1959. 'I give Castro a year,' he said. 'No more.' Batista died in 1973; Castro was still ruling Cuba into the twenty-first century.

❖

The former owner of the *Daily Express*, Lord Beaverbrook, refused to employ Winston Churchill in 1932, declaring that the politician, historian and prolific writer was a 'busted flush'.

In 1939 Beaverbrook went even further. 'This man Churchill is the enemy of the British Empire,' the noble Lord insisted. 'This man Churchill is a warmonger. He is turning the thoughts of the British Empire to war. He must be stopped.'

Not long afterward Churchill became Prime Minster in a war-time coalition government and helped lead Britain and the Allies to victory over Nazi Germany.

Perhaps to make amends, the press baron insisted in 1945 that Churchill would lead the Conservatives to victory in the imminent General Election. It was in fact a Labour landslide and Clem Attlee became Prime Minister.

❖

When the soldier and former heavyweight boxer Idi Amin seized power in Uganda in 1971, sections of the British press fell over themselves to heap praise on the dictator. The *Daily Telegraph* described the 'General' as a 'model of self-restraint' while the *Daily Express* believed him capable of 'running a smooth administration'. *The Times* stated: 'One feels that Uganda cannot afford General Amin's warm-hearted generosity'. This was the same Amin who soon afterwards expelled all Asians from his country and presided over a reign of terror over his people until 1979, when he was forced to flee in disgrace.

❖

Marxism may now be largely discredited in governments throughout the world, but an obituary of its originator Karl Marx in St Petersburg, Russia, in March 1883 was a little premature. It announced: 'Marx's audacious attempt to destroy the basis of contemporary society with the aid of what seemed to be the cardinal principles of political economy has utterly failed.'

Another obituary, this time in Austria, said: 'The damage Marx created will pass like a corpse.'

While a third notice, this one in California, stated: 'The socialist ideas which he had tried to propagate failed to make a lasting impression.'

Within forty years the Soviet Union was in place, basing its philosophy firmly upon Marx's teachings.

❖

The former Liberal Prime Minister and statesman David Lloyd George was deeply pessimistic in 1936 about the outcome of any new war in Europe. 'Democracy will never survive another world war,' the Welshman stated, three years before the Second World War, which ultimately strengthened democracy's grip in Western Europe.

❖

The Prime Minister of Rhodesia – now Zimbabwe – Ian Smith announced in 1967 that: 'I think Rhodesia is a model for the rest of the world so far as race relations are concerned. I know of no happier country.' In 1971 he added: 'We have the happiest Africans in the world.' The country was soon in the grip of a bitter civil war.

◈

The American journalist William Allen White stated in 1899:
'Only Anglo-Saxons can govern themselves.'

◈

Despite the onset of the Great Depression in the early 1930s,
the election of Democrat Franklin D. Roosevelt over the
Republican incumbent Herbert Hoover was not predicted by
everyone. In November 1932 an opinion poll carried out by
Hearst publications and reported in the *New York Times*
claimed that Hoover would win by four electoral college votes.
In fact, Roosevelt took that election with the stunning margin
of 472 electoral college votes to 59.

◈

Once F. D. R. had been elected in 1932, it was not long before
many political 'experts' were writing him off. The *New York
Herald Tribune* columnist Mark Sullivan declared: 'F. D. R. will
be a one-term president.' The American critic H. L. Mencken
believed in 1936 that his opponents could beat Roosevelt 'with
a Chinaman or even a Republican'.

And the famous publishing magnate William Randolph
Hearst said he would 'stake my reputation as a prophet' that
Roosevelt would lose the 1936 election.

The critics were all a little hasty to write the end of
F. D. R.'s career. He not only won in 1936, but again in 1940,
and also in 1944. The only way, it seemed, to get F. D. R. out of
office was in a coffin – he died in 1945.

◈

The optimism – not to say blind optimism – of politicians can
sometimes take the breath away. In 1968 Tony Benn, then a
leading figure in the Labour Government, suggested: 'We

thought we could put the economy right in five years. We were
wrong. It will probably take ten.'

❖

Bill Clinton was not only known as the Comeback Kid – he
made a mockery of most political predictions. In 1991 a senior
Washington columnist, Geoffrey Sperling Jnr, stated: 'All
indications are that Bush [George senior] is unbeatable.' By
February 1992 a Democratic poll expert Alan Secrest had
concluded: 'Clinton's candidacy is irretrievable.' To be followed
by another Democratic pollster Tubby Harrison who said in
May 1992: 'Clinton is a dead stone loser'.

The man from Arkansas won the next two presidential
elections.

❖

The end to the capitalist system has long been predicted by
observers. An American journalist called Lincoln Steffens
visited Russia in 1919 when the Communist Revolution was
establishing itself across that vast country. He said simply: 'I
have been into the future and it works.'

More directly still the Soviet premier, as he then was, Nikita
Khrushchev, told Western diplomats in Moscow in 1956:
'Whether you like it or not, history is on our side. We will bury
you.'

History was in fact on the side of the West – with the fall of
the Berlin wall in 1989 heralding the end of communism
throughout Eastern Europe and ultimately Russia and the
former Soviet states.

❖

The journalist Curt Reiss, writing in 1942, insisted that
General Charles de Gaulle – the head of the Free French

during the Second World War – was a soldier through and through with no desire to be a future leader of his country. 'De Gaulle has no political ambitions whatsoever,' wrote Reiss. 'Once victory is achieved, he wants to step down and be once more what he has always been and always will be – a soldier.'

In 1958 De Gaulle became the President of France, a post he retained for eleven years.

When Adolf Hitler's nephew Willie visited Britain in 1937, the 26-year-old insisted: 'My uncle is a peaceful man. He thinks war is not worth the candle.' Within two years the world was at war with Germany.

The clamour over suspected 'Reds under the bed' in the United States in the 1950s led to some curious pronouncements. A Senator from Indiana, William E. Jenner was convinced that the battle was already almost lost. He said in 1951: 'This country is today in the hands of a secret inner coterie…which is directed by agents of the Soviet Union.' The country's only choice, he said, was to impeach President Harry Truman to find out who was in this 'secret invisible government'.

The infamous Joseph McCarthy, a Senator from Wisconsin and self-appointed hunter of communists, believed that the 'present situation' in the United States was caused by one thing, and one thing only. 'This must be the product of a great conspiracy, a conspiracy on a scale so immense as to dwarf any previous venture in the history of man.'

McCarthy initially claimed to have a list of no fewer than 205 officials in the Department of State who were members of

the Communist Party. This was reduced to one, a man called
Owen Lattimore, whom McCarthy described as 'the top
Russian espionage agent in the country'. McCarthy said he
staked his reputation on the claim.

Lattimore, who denied the accusation, was charged with
perjury and found not guilty on all charges by 1955. The
greatest conspiracy in the 'history of mankind' had not, it
seemed, existed after all.

Never the brightest of politicians, President Gerald Ford
showed himself up with a particularly bizarre prediction while
debating with Democratic candidate Jimmy Carter in the 1976
race for the White House. 'There is no Soviet domination of
Eastern Europe and there never will be under a Ford
administration.' Eastern Europe had of course been part of the
Soviet bloc since just after the Second World War and was to
remain so until the Berlin Wall came down in 1989. Perhaps it
was no surprise when Carter won the election.

Well, even politicians are allowed to change their minds – even
if some of us might wish they hadn't. The former actor and
Governor of California Ronald Reagan said in 1973: 'The
thought of being President frightens me and I do not think I
want the job.' Eight years later he was behind the desk in the
Oval Office at the White House.

The Labour politician Shirley Williams announced in May
1980 that she firmly planned to stay in the party. 'I am not
interested in a third party. I do not believe that it has any
future.' In 1981, as one of the so-called Gang of Four, Williams
helped found the Social Democratic Party. In one sense she

had been right, the new party did not have a future – it finally folded in 1990 after most of its members had merged with the Liberals.

# Grave Predictions

*And finally. Death may be no joking matter, but there's something deeply fascinating about how other people foresee – or often don't foresee – their own ends. That's the secret of why we enjoy this fascinating area of predictions – it's about other people's deaths and not our own. After all, as the comedian Woody Allen says, he's not worried about death – he just doesn't want to be there when it happens. So at the time these remarks may have not been intended to make us laugh, but now with the benefit of hindsight, it's hard to resist a wry chuckle or at least a little shiver at the realisation of our own mortality.*

It was 1864, the American Civil War was raging and the scene was the Battle of Spotsylvania. The Union's General John Sedgwick referring to the enemy's snipers said: 'They couldn't hit an elephant at this distance.' The next moment he was dead – killed by an enemy sniper.

Just occasionally you have to feel sorry for newspapers. In May 1974, the *Bath and West Evening Chronicle* wrote that the bandleader Duke Ellington 'seemed destined to go on forever'. The very next day the sad news was announced of the Duke's death in New York.

A Zambian magician called Lemmy Chipowe once announced a new trick in which he asked his audience to bury him in the ground for two and a half hours before digging him up again. 'Don't worry,' he told them, 'I'll still be breathing.' So Chipowe lay down in the makeshift grave while the audience covered him with earth. Two and a half hours later they did as they were told and dug the magician up – only to find Chipowe was dead. Even worse, he had made them pay in advance.

Robert Francis Kennedy, or 'Bobby' as he was commonly known, made what turned out to be a chilling statement in 1967 when he said: 'Who knows if any of us will be around in 1972. Fate is so fickle.' The next year, while campaigning for the Democratic nomination in the US Presidential election, he was assassinated in California. It was the fate which had befallen his brother John (J. F. K.) five years earlier when he was President.

In the ancient world a Greek by the name of Calchas was informed by a seer – someone who could see into the future – that on a given date he would die from laughter. When the appointed day arrived Calchas was amused that, contrary to the seer's prophesy, he was in fact alive and kicking. In fact he found the whole idea so amusing that he started to giggle, then to laugh, and finally began to roar with laughter. At which he dropped down dead.

One Anthony J. Drexel III, a member of a very prominent and wealthy New York family, was one day showing guests the contents of the gun room when he picked up an unfamiliar weapon. 'Look here's one you haven't seen before,' he told the visitors before airily waving the gun in the air and pulling the trigger. He shot himself dead.

Back in 1971 a spokesman for the Astrological Association came up with these predictions for the future. 'By 1980 people will not be eating meat. This is possibly connected with some kind of blight on the animals or the fact that they might be uneconomic to harvest. I have a horrible feeling that edible animals are not going to be alive in 1980. In thirty years we will have a TV set with which to communicate with the dead.'

The bandleader Glenn Miller seemed to be aware of potential calamity ahead when he stepped on board the plane that was to take him from England to France in December 1944. 'Hey, where are the parachutes?' he was heard to remark. The reported reply from friend and fellow passenger USAF Major

Norman Baessell was even more chilling. 'What's the matter, Miller?' he shouted. 'Do you want to live forever?' The plane left for Paris and was never seen again. No bodies or wreckage were ever found.

A Hungarian hypnotist was putting on a show at the town of Izsak in 1936. Part of the act was to get someone from the audience to come up on stage and act as a volunteer to help show off the hypnotist's skills. On this occasion a powerful young farmer by the name of Karoly Szani stepped forward to join in the act.

Before long the farmer was deep in a trance and the hypnotist started the routine. 'Here's a knife,' he told Szani. 'Take it and stand up – here comes one of your enemies. You hate him because he has stolen your sweetheart!'

The audience was rapt with attention as the farmer showed his anger, and the hypnotist kept developing the theme. 'Watch out!' he told Szani. 'Your enemy is about to attack you! Get him!'

These were the last words the hypnotist uttered. At this command the young farmer leapt forward and stabbed the hypnotist hard in the chest, puncturing his heart. As the performer was taken dying to hospital, a medic brought Szani out of his hypnotic trance. He, of course, had no idea what had happened.

The year was 1861 and a US Senator from Michigan named Zachariah Chandler was making known his views on the growing tension between the Union north and the Confederate south of the country. He declared: 'A little bloodletting might be necessary.'

Four years later this 'little bloodletting' or the American

Civil War, as it is more often called, had left more than 600,000 troops dead and cost the country some $20 billion.

❖

Nellie Connally, wife of the then Governor of Texas John Connally, was travelling with the Democratic president John F. Kennedy on that fateful day of 22 November 1963. As the motorcade proceeded through the cheering crowds in Dallas Mrs Connally turned to J. F. K. and said: 'Mr. President, you certainly cannot say that Dallas does not love you.' Moments later the President was hit by sniper fire and died a short time later.

On that morning, the *Daily Express* newspaper had carried a photo of J. F. K.'s main political rival, the Republican Barry Goldwater. The caption ran: 'The Man who is Gunning for Kennedy'.

❖

President Gerald Ford once exclaimed: 'If Lincoln were living today, he would turn over in his grave!'

❖

A corrupt sheriff, Henry Plummer, asked the townsfolk of Bannock, Washington, in 1864: 'You wouldn't hang your own sheriff, would you?' They would – and they did.

❖

The Republican Senator from Utah, Orrin Hatch, once said: 'Capital punishment is our society's recognition of the sanctity of human life.'

❖

Schoolteacher Harry Johnson was the toast of Britain when, in 1979, at the age of 59, he won more than £750,000 on the football pools. The Manchester teacher planned a few luxuries

ahead – a cruise, new home, a new car – but unfortunately fell
ill shortly afterwards with a mystery illness. He said: 'My God,
I've won all this money. I hope I'm not going to kick the bucket
before I can spend some of it.' Sadly, Harry did just that – only
six weeks after winning the money.

※

A member of a Texas pesticide review board, Othal Brand,
once said of the pesticide Chlordane: 'Sure, it's going to kill a
lot of people, but they may be dying of something else anyway.'

※

Giving yourself, or your group, a name can sometimes be
tempting fate. That was the experience of three popular
evangelical preachers in Africa who called themselves 'God's
Favourite Children'. The name perhaps took on a slightly
different meaning when the three were appearing at an open
air service in Oyo, Nigeria, and a lightning strike killed all
'God's Favourite Children' on the spot.

※

In April 1918, the great war ace of the First World War, the
German Baron Manfred von Richthofen, was amused by the
insistence of an autograph hunter who wanted the famous
flyer's signature. As the Red Baron clambered into his
trademark red Fokker Triplane, he asked his fan: 'Don't you
think I'll come back?' Perhaps the fan had a premonition,
because within a few hours Richthofen was involved in a
deadly aerial battle with an Allied pilot, and crashed and died.

※

The great circus act and high-wire walker Karl Wallenda was
73 and still walking tall when he attempted to walk across a
300 ft long wire between two buildings in San Juan, Puerto

Rico in March 1978. The wire was 100 ft in the air but the great man appeared undaunted. 'The wind is stronger in the street than it is up here,' he shouted as he began to walk across. Then a sudden gust of wind unsettled him and Wallenda fell to the ground to his death.

A light aircraft crashed in April 1974, killing the two passengers, Todd Missfield and Bonnie Johnson. According to a Canadian newspaper, the plane had crashed into a billboard proclaiming the words: 'Learn to Fly'.

Captain Oates left his colleagues' tent on Robert Scott's expedition to the Antarctic in 1912 and said softly: 'I am just going outside. I may be some time.' He was. Oates, who had been suffering from frostbite, sacrificed himself rather than hold the expedition up, and never returned to the tent.

The drummer for The Who rock band, Keith Moon, lived a typical kind of rocker's life in his youth, but by 1977 he claimed to have got that out of his system. He said then: 'I think we just sort of grew out of drugs, the drugs aren't necessary any more.' The following year Moon died, from a drugs and alcohol overdose.

It isn't hard to feel sympathy for the fate of Elizabeth McClelland, who in 1978 at the decent age of 78, decided she had had enough of the growing civil unrest of her native Belfast in Northern Ireland. She upped and emigrated to the more tranquil surroundings of Christchurch in New Zealand. 'I want to get away from all the street violence,' she said. Sadly,

Mrs McClelland died in a hospital in her adopted homeland. She had been hit over the head during a demonstration by a placard proclaiming Irish Civil Rights.

The great British Foreign Secretary and Prime Minister Lord Palmerston lay dying in 1865. His last recorded words were: 'Die, my dear doctor? That's the last thing I shall do.'

Irate passenger Alfred Lewis lost the plot when he missed his stop on a Chicago Transit Authority bus in 1972 and the driver refused to let him off the vehicle before they reached the next stop some way off. 'I'm gonna get off the bus if I have to blast my way off,' shouted Lewis, whereupon he pulled out a handgun. What he didn't reckon on was that another passenger was armed too, and he pulled out his pistol. In the shoot-out that ensued, seven people were injured and one man was killed. That man was Alfred Lewis, who finally got to leave the bus – dead.

Someone in the US army clearly thought they were onto a winner with the slogan 'Patriotism is Life' at a local exhibition of troops stationed in Germany in 1978. The culmination of the event was to see one Sergeant George McGraw dropping in by parachute, proudly holding the Stars and Stripes flag to underline the slogan's meaning. The impact of this bravura display was slightly altered however when on descent Sgt McGraw's parachute became tangled up with the flag, causing him to plunge into a nearby cemetery to his very own patriotic death.

The impending eruption of Mount St Helens in Washington State in the US was understandably causing nervousness among local residents. All except, that is, a stubborn 83-year-old called Harry Truman. Truman had lived on the mountain's slopes for half a century and perhaps understandably felt he knew it better than most people. As the media gathered and neighbours left for safety, Truman insisted that the volcanic mountain was not able to get out of hand. 'No one knows more about this mountain than Harry,' he said. 'This goddamned mountain won't blow.' And in a wonderfully inventive side swipe at the experts he declared: 'Scientists don't know shit from apple butter!' So he holed up with his cats and plenty of whisky to see the episode out. Alas for Harry, the scientists on this occasion did know their apple butter, and on 18 May 1980, the mountain blew with devastating force, obliterating Harry, his home and cats. Locals later reckoned his last recorded words were: 'My God, they were right!'

In 1976 one D. H. Beenan from New Zealand was so opposed to capital punishment that he wanted to demonstrate the full horror of hanging to his friends. With his fiancée Bebe Trumper among those watching, Beenan stood on a chair and put a noose around his neck. He told the startled onlookers: 'How horrible the whole thing is.' With that Beenan leapt off the chair and hanged himself to death.

The lead singer of the pop group Chicago, Terry Kath, thought he knew a thing or two about guns, and was a collector. After a party in January 1978, Kath began playing with a couple of weapons. First he put a revolver to his head, pulled the trigger and 'click' – he knew it was not loaded. Then he picked up an automatic handgun to repeat the trick. A friend tried to dissuade him, but Kath removed the clip from the gun and said: 'Don't worry, it's not loaded.' What Kath had forgotten was that with a gun of this type a bullet is automatically put into the chamber and stays there even if the clip is removed. So when Kath pulled the trigger this time there was more than a 'click'.

The controversial former British politician Ramsay MacDonald, the first Labour Prime Minister, set out for a cruise to South America in November 1937 after the end of his political career. When asked about his future plans he replied: 'I have no plans. I am in search of that most elusive of all forms of happiness – rest.'

MacDonald certainly got what he was looking for though perhaps not in the way he had foreseen – five days later he died at sea.

Viscount Templewood had a jolly view of British Society when writing in 1951. 'Executions are so much part of British history that it is almost impossible for many excellent people to think of the future without them.' The last executions in Britain occurred in August 1964.

The Mayor of San Francisco George Moscone said in a magazine interview in 1976 : 'I hate to say it, but crime is an overhead you have to pay if you want to live in the city.' How right he was. The mayor was later shot and killed in his office by a former policeman with a grudge.

Earl Mountbatten, the last Viceroy of India, was dismissive of suggestions that he might become a target for terrorist organisations such as the IRA later in his life. In 1978 the 78-year-old retired admiral asked: 'What would they want with an old man like me?'

A year later on 27 August, Mountbatten was killed while sailing his yacht near his holiday home in Ireland – the victim of an IRA bomb.

The President of Korea, President Park Chung Hee, was shot while having dinner in 1979 by one of his own bodyguards. Two women present bent over the ailing politician and demanded: 'Are you all right, Excellency?'

The President looked up at them and replied: 'I am all right.' They were the final words he uttered.

As the renowned wit and first woman MP in the House of Commons, Lady Nancy Astor, lay dying in 1964, her family surrounded her bed to comfort her in those last moments. Suddenly she awoke from her slumber to murmur: 'Am I dying or is this my birthday?'

Those were her final words.